DATE DUE

Scott O'Dell

Twayne's United States Authors Series

Ruth MacDonald, Editor

TUSAS 710

SCOTT O'DELL.
Courtesy of Houghton Mifflin Company.

Scott O'Dell

David L. Russell

Ferris State University

Twayne Publishers
New York

Twayne's United States Authors Series No. 710

Scott O'Dell
David L. Russell

Twayne Publishers
1633 Broadway
New York, NY 10019

Library of Congress Cataloging-in-Publication Data

Russell, David L., 1946–
    Scott O'Dell / David L. Russell.
       p.   cm. — (Twayne's United States author series ; TUSAS 710)
    Includes bibliographical references and index.
    ISBN 0-8057-1682-3 (alk. paper)
    1. O'Dell, Scott, 1898–1989—Criticism and interpretation.
  2. Historical fiction, American—History and criticism.
  3. Children's stories, American—History and criticism.   I. Title.
  II. Series.
    PS3529.D434Z78   1999
813'.54—dc21   99-19718
 [B]   CIP

For Jennifer, Megan, and Elizabeth, with love.

Contents

Preface

By any measure, Scott O'Dell must be considered a major figure in the children's literature of the latter half of the twentieth century. On the strength of *Island of the Blue Dolphins* alone O'Dell could claim an exalted place in the hierarchy of great children's authors. When we add to that such noteworthy volumes as *The King's Fifth, The Black Pearl,* and *Sing Down the Moon,* his accomplishment becomes quite remarkable. His books have been showered with awards, translated into foreign languages, and remain today, decades after their first appearance, widely read and admired. It is, in fact, surprising that a full-length study of O'Dell's works has not appeared before this.

This work treats all of O'Dell's major writings, including his books for adults (he wrote exclusively for adults until he was past 60). However, it is as a children's writer that he will be remembered, and the primary emphasis in this study is on the children's books. The study is largely organized by chronology, beginning with O'Dell's earliest writings (those for adults) and ending with his last novel (completed by his widow, Elizabeth Hall), *Thunder Rolling in the Mountains.* I have departed from a strict chronological discussion of the works when it seemed logical and appropriate. Chapter 4, for example, is devoted to his works about the Old Southwest, including Spanish Mexico. Chapter 5 examines works of the early 1970s, during which time O'Dell was experimenting with books for younger readers, a memoir/travelogue, and historical novels focusing on different times and places. In the later 1970s O'Dell began to write contemporary fiction, and all these books have been grouped together in chapter 7. Chapter 8 discusses his final works of historical fiction, spanning most of the 1980s. It is hoped that this organization will provide the reader with a sense of O'Dell's development as a writer as well as give some unity to the potentially disparate discussions in the various chapters.

In some respects, it could be argued that O'Dell developed little as a writer of children's stories after the publication of his first two or three in the early 1960s. He certainly never wrote anything as critically acclaimed or as well received as his early books for children. He experimented, as has been suggested above, in a variety of forms in the 1970s and 1980s, but he would produce nothing with such happy results as he had with his early historical fiction. But, to be sure, O'Dell had two tough acts to follow in *Island of the Blue Dolphins* and *The King's Fifth*. If he seemed to develop little as a writer of children's books during his career, we must not forget that he began that career fairly well at the top. Few authors have produced a Newbery Medal winner and three Newbery Honor Award books in the entire body of their work, let alone in the first decade of their careers. Ultimately it will be these works on which O'Dell must and should be judged.

As with any work of this sort, I have sought a great deal of help from others. I wish to thank Scott O'Dell's colleagues and friends who kindly assisted me, including his longtime friend and first editor at Houghton Mifflin, Mr. Austin Olney, and his wife, Marcia Legru, and Ms. Matilda Welter, his longtime editor at Houghton-Mifflin. But this book would not at all have been possible without the generosity and kindness of Scott O'Dell's widow, Elizabeth Hall, who provided me with invaluable insights, welcomed me into her home, and endured countless telephone calls and letters. I shall never forget her graciousness.

Of course, I must assume full responsibility for the contents of this work. I trust that my praise has been tempered with good judgment and my censure with goodwill, and that the whole is a worthy tribute to the author of *Island of the Blue Dolphins*.

Chronology

1898	Odell Gabriel Scott born 23 May in Los Angeles, son of Bennett Mason and May Elizabeth (Gabriel) Scott.
1918	Inducted into U.S. Army 9 October; discharged 17 December.
1919	Attends Occidental College.
1920	Attends University of Wisconsin.
1920–1921	Attends Stanford University.
Early 1920s	Set dresser and eventually technical director for Paramount Pictures; writes occasional articles; inspired by a newspaper copyist's error that transposed his name, changes name to Scott O'Dell.
1924	First published book, *Representative Photoplays Analyzed*, appears.
Mid-1920s	Cameraman for Metro-Goldwyn-Mayer; works on *Ben Hur, Son of the Sheik,* and other silent films.
1925	Attends University of Rome briefly and lives for a year in Florence; writes first (never-published) novel, *Pinfeathers*.
ca. 1927	Returns to United States; continues to write; speculates in oil and other ventures.
1934	First published novel, *Woman of Spain: A Story of Old California*, appears.
Mid-1930s	Dabbles in citrus ranching; lives off proceeds from *Woman of Spain*.
1942–1943	Enlists in U.S. Air Force, 22 September 1942; discharged 1 April 1943; serves in Coast Guard Auxiliary for duration of World War II.
1948	Marries Jane Dorsa Rattenbury in Santa Barbara, California.
1947–1955	Book editor for *Los Angeles Daily News*.

1960   Publishes first young people's novel, *Island of the Blue Dolphins*; receives Rupert Hughes Award (*Island of the Blue Dolphins*).

1961   Receives Newbery Medal, Lewis Carroll Shelf Award, and Southern California Council on Literature for Children and Young People Notable Book Award (*Island of the Blue Dolphins*).

1962   Receives Hans Christian Andersen Award of Merit from the International Board on Books for Young People (*Island of the Blue Dolphins*).

1963   Receives William Allen White Award and German Juvenile International Award (*Island of the Blue Dolphins*).

1964   Receives Nene Award from the Hawaii Library Association (*Island of the Blue Dolphins*).

1966   Separates from first wife.

1967   Moves to Corona del Mar, California, with Elizabeth Hall, his second wife; Newbery Honor book (*The King's Fifth*).

1968   Receives German Juvenile International Award (*The King's Fifth*); *The Black Pearl* is named Newbery Honor book; receives George A. Stone Center for Children's Books, Claremont Graduate School, Recognition of Merit (*Island of the Blue Dolphins*).

1970   Moves to Rancho Santa Fe, California.

1971   *Sing Down the Moon* is named Newbery Honor book.

1972   Receives Hans Christian Andersen Medal for the body of his work.

1975   O'Dell and Hall move from California to New York state, where she becomes managing editor of *Psychology Today*.

1976   Receives University of Southern Mississippi Award for the body of his work.

1978   Receives Catholic Library Association Regina Medal for the body of his work.

1981   Receives FOCAL Award, Los Angeles Public Library (*Island of the Blue Dolphins*).

1984   Establishes Scott O'Dell Award for Historical Fiction; receives Parents' Choice Award (*Alexandra*).

1985   Receives OMAR Award (*Island of the Blue Dolphins*) and Florida State Historical Association Award (*Alexandra*).

1986   Receives Parents' Choice Award (*Streams to the River, River to the Sea*).

1987   Receives O'Dell Award for Historical Fiction (*Streams to the River, River to the Sea*).

1989   Receives Children's Literature Award, School Media Specialists of Southeastern New York, for the body of his work.

1989   Dies, 15 October, Mount Kisco, New York.

1990   *Sing Down the Moon* named Phoenix Award Honor book, Children's Literature Association.

Chapter One

The Life and Times of Scott O'Dell

No educated person . . . can live a complete life
without a knowledge of where we come from.
— O'Dell, quoted in *Something about the Author* (1990)

Scott O'Dell—probably the foremost American writer of children's historical fiction of the latter half of the twentieth century—was over 60 years old before he wrote a single word for children. In fact, had he died before turning 60, he would be a decidedly minor literary figure. A writer all his life, his career had been rather lackluster, his publications sporadic, his literary achievements of little note. However, in 1960, he ventured into unexplored territory with the publication of his first novel for young people, *Island of the Blue Dolphins.* Few children's authors can claim such instant success. The book won the coveted Newbery Medal for most distinguished children's book of 1960, as well as a myriad of other national and international awards, and it is one of the most enduring children's books of the twentieth century.

But O'Dell was not to prove a "one-hit wonder." Following the success of *Island of the Blue Dolphins,* he turned his energies almost exclusively to writing for young audiences. Although it would be another six years before his next book, *The King's Fifth,* appeared, that work was named a Newbery Honor book as was his next, *The Black Pearl,* which appeared just one year later. These books established O'Dell's reputation as a writer of first-rate historical fiction. His final Newbery Honor book, *Sing Down the Moon,* appeared in 1971. In 1972, he received the prestigious Hans Christian Andersen Award for the significant international contribution of the body of his work—he was only the second American author to have been so honored. (The first was Meindert DeJong, who won the award in 1962. The American artist Maurice Sendak received the 1970 Hans Christian Andersen Award for illustration.) The remarkable success of his first 10 years as a children's writer would be difficult for anyone to sustain, and much of O'Dell's later works receive the attention they do largely because he wrote them. Nevertheless, by any standard, Scott O'Dell is one of the principal figures in twentieth-century American young people's fiction. He revitalized a

1

form that had fallen out of favor in the post–World War II era—that of historical fiction for young people. And he sought to raise the social conscience of young readers by introducing themes largely ignored by earlier writers, including the reprehensible treatment of indigenous peoples in America by the invading Europeans, the corruption of civilization by humanity's greed and lust for power, the importance of an ecological understanding of human existence, and the recognition of gender equality through the portrayal of strong female protagonists. If O'Dell's work has occasionally met with criticism—he was not a great stylist, his plots do not always hold together, his characters are at times thinly developed—we should not forget that his efforts are those of a pioneer. It may be enough that he blazed a trail; we need not expect that he should pave it as well.

Early accounts of O'Dell's life typically contain two glaring errors—the date of his birth and his birth name. He was born Odell Gabriel Scott in Los Angeles, California, on 23 May 1898. Until the 1980s, most reference works cited his year of birth as 1903—an error that he apparently condoned and perhaps promulgated. A typesetter's error would prompt Odell Scott to become Scott O'Dell. He was the only son of Bennett Mason Scott and May Elizabeth (Gabriel) Scott; his only sibling, his sister Lucile, was several years younger than he. By a happy coincidence, his great-grandmother was a first cousin of Sir Walter Scott, the father of the English historical novel, the same genre in which O'Dell would distinguish himself. The Scotts were originally from Columbus, Ohio, his mother having been born there, but they settled in southern California, where his father worked, for a time, as an official of the Union Pacific Railroad. The family moved several times during his youth, although never very far from the Los Angeles area. Eventually, when O'Dell was older, his father owned two drug stores in downtown Los Angeles.

O'Dell's own recollections of his father were not especially happy ones: "My father was an autocrat who couldn't care less about his children. I never had a good relationship with him. . . ."[1] It is not surprising that among the stories O'Dell fondly remembered from his childhood were *Treasure Island* and the folktale "Jack and the Beanstalk," both of which depict fatherless sons.[2] It is tempting to speculate how much this unhappy relationship contributed to the portraits of overbearing and willful fathers that appear in such works as *Carlota* or *The Spanish Smile*.

The southern California of O'Dell's youth was a rugged and undeveloped outpost. O'Dell once remarked that "Los Angeles was a frontier town when I was born there. It had more horses than automobiles and more jackrabbits than people. The first sound I remember was a wildcat scratching on the roof of our house."[3] His memories of his early life in California influenced his writings throughout his life, and the Old Southwest became a favorite setting for O'Dell, one that he returned to many times. For a time, the family lived by the ocean in San Pedro in a house built on stilts. Certainly this experience contributed to his lifelong love of the sea, which plays so important a role in many of his works both for adults and children. Odell also enjoyed happy childhood experiences living in Julian near the Mexican border "in the heart of the Oriflamme Mountains, the ancestral home of the Diegueno Indians." It is to this part of his life that he attributes his interest in "Indians, Spaniards, and Mexicans."[4]

One childhood experience was embedded in his memory for life. He tells of going with his companions

> into the Palos Verdes Hills. There we turned over every likely rock, looking for small monsters. We thrust our hands down every squirrel and coyote hole in our path. Commonly we found an owl. This was the prize of all prizes. It was twice the size of your fist, soft-feathered, with great yellow eyes that blinked in the sudden sun.
>
> What did we do with this creature of the nocturnal air? We killed it, of course. We wrung its neck. We cut off its legs. For the exposed tendons of an owl's legs, when pulled in a certain way, made the tiny claws open and retract in a ghastly simulation of life.
>
> To this day, indeed to this very minute, I remember these depredations with horror. (Commire, 114)

We can recognize in this account one of the roots of the adult O'Dell's abhorrence of the violence that humans perpetrate on the natural world, a conviction that would find its surest and most powerful expression in the actions of Karana, the heroine of *Island of the Blue Dolphins*.

O'Dell's early formal education had little impact on him, but he always enjoyed reading. When he was 10, his parents gave him the works of his ancestor Sir Walter Scott, and he fell in love with them. Perhaps from that time forward he was destined to be a historical novelist himself, but the path would be long and circuitous.

O'Dell attended Long Beach Polytechnic High School in Long Beach, California, and was inducted into the U.S. Army on 9 October 1918. The army sent him to Occidental College in Los Angeles for officer's training, but with the declaration of the armistice on 11 November, he was no longer needed and was discharged on 17 December 1918. He remained at Occidental for the following term to pursue academic studies. This brief foray into academia was followed with stints at the University of Wisconsin and at Stanford University, but he never received a degree; indeed he never completed more than a single year at any college. He was frustrated that the college curriculum did not seem to be helping him learn to write—for by that time he had determined to become a writer. He enjoyed taking the courses he wanted to take— "psychology, philosophy, history, and English"—but his education lacked direction and he finally abandoned formal schooling altogether (quoted in Commire, 114). He did boast one accomplishment during his sporadic college career and that was, during his brief stay at the University of Wisconsin, introducing Charles Rawlings to Marjorie Kinnan. The couple eventually married and Marjorie Kinnan Rawlings would make her own name in children's literature as the author of the beloved animal classic *The Yearling*.[5]

Having abandoned his quest for a college degree, O'Dell decided simply to begin writing. He soon sold several articles on a variety of subjects to local newspapers, and it was for one of these first publications that a printer mistakenly transposed his name, producing the byline "Scott O'Dell." He immediately recognized the more mellifluous name and believed it sounded more like a writer's. He decided to be henceforth known as Scott O'Dell and had his name legally changed. One of O'Dell's first jobs was with the Palmer Photoplay Company, perhaps as early as 1918 or 1919, where he read and critiqued photoplays intended for silent movies. Eventually he began to teach a mail-order course in photoplay writing. This led to his first published book-length work, *Representative Photoplays Analyzed* (1924), which he wrote while he worked as a technical director for the Paramount Motion Picture Studio, a job he held from 1924 to 1925. The motion picture business fascinated him in those early years—although he would lose almost all interest in film in later life. In those formative Hollywood years, he worked with such luminaries as Gloria Swanson and Rudolph Valentino, and, in fact, became one of the earliest hand models. During the filming of *Son of the Sheik*, Valentino's last movie, a scene called for a close-up of Valentino's hands fingering a strand of pearls. But Valentino had "the hands of a butcher," and O'Dell recalls that "somebody happened to notice my hands. I was very slender then, young, and I had very aesthetic, long fingers. So they chose me to hold the pearls, and that was my only acting occasion."[6] He also worked for Metro-Goldwyn-Mayer and was the second cameraman for the original motion picture of *Ben Hur* on location in Italy. He recalls "carrying the first Technicolor camera, made by hand at M.I.T., around the Roman countryside" (Commire, 114). While in Italy, he briefly attended the University of Rome, but, as with all his other scholastic forays, he left without a degree. It was also on this assignment that O'Dell met and formed a lasting friendship with John Barrymore. Through Barrymore, O'Dell came to know most of the influential people in the film industry, and for a long time he would be part of that Hollywood set. His experiences in Rome included a police arrest with F. Scott Fitzgerald (the details are vague, but the event is not out of keeping with the lifestyle O'Dell was used to during this period).

O'Dell remained in Italy after the film company returned to the States, and, while living in Florence (in a villa once occupied by Galileo), he wrote *Pinfeathers,* his first novel, which was never published. He was later to remark that the work was appropriately named "because it was very young and fuzzy" ("Dignity," 184). Following his return to the United States in about 1927, O'Dell found further work in the movies, continued his writing, and speculated in California oil properties. Employment seems to have been erratic for O'Dell, and during one particularly desperate period, he made ends meet "by sitting in his stockbroker's office all day, watching the ticker, and moving in and out of the market."[7] He also tried his hand at citrus farming, at which he was engaged while writing what was to be his first published novel, *Woman of Spain: A Story of Old California,* which appeared in 1934.

Greta Garbo persuaded MGM to buy the rights to O'Dell's *Woman of Spain* for $24,000, a windfall that provided a very comfortable living for O'Dell throughout the Great Depression. The 1930s must have been a lively decade for O'Dell, if not one particularly conducive to serious writing; he had a large cadre of friends in the motion picture business. He caroused with John Barrymore, who called him "Mercutio." It was also during the thirties that O'Dell introduced his friend Raoul Schumacher to the celebrity aviator Beryl Markham, and the couple eventually married. After she married Schumacher, Markham penned her famous memoir *West with the Night.* The book was to encounter considerable controversy much later, with O'Dell in the thick of it. O'Dell had always believed that *West with the Night* was principally Schumacher's work, and in a letter to *Vanity Fair* in 1987 he openly said so.[8] Such experiences reveal the high living O'Dell enjoyed in the 1930s and 1940s.

On 22 September 1942, when he was 44 years old, O'Dell enlisted in the U.S. Air Force—perhaps to avoid the draft, for O'Dell had no dependents and had failed in his attempts to get a commission to do public relations work for the military. He was sent to Sheppard Field, Texas, where he reviewed the IQ tests of inductees and recommended service assignments for them. When the air force learned that O'Dell's own IQ was 140, he was sent to upstate New York to learn cryptography—"the last thing in the world he wanted to do," according to his wife.[9] He managed to wrangle a discharge on 1 April 1943 to "go into essential industry." He spent the remainder of the war in the Coast Guard Auxiliary and often went out in a small boat on night patrols along the California coast—occasionally accompanied by his co-volunteer, Humphrey Bogart.

In 1947 his second published novel, *Hill of the Hawk,* appeared. The story is set in California during the Mexican War, a favorite setting of his and one that he would return to in a book for young readers. He would even use many of the same character names—although the characters themselves would be different—and some of the same episodes. The dust jacket biography on *Hill of the Hawk* identifies O'Dell as still a bachelor and a citrus farmer. But it is around this time that he sold the ranch to a developer, noting that was the only way a citrus rancher could make any money (his allowing the land to be developed is rather ironic given his pro-environment stands in his later writings). At the time of *Hill of the Hawk's* publication O'Dell took a job as the book editor for the *Los Angeles Daily News* and contributed occasional articles to other periodicals.

On 29 April 1948, O'Dell was married to Jane Dorsa Rattenbury. Theirs seems to have been rocky relationship, although from the beginning the couple maintained a lively social schedule, counting among their acquaintances the Hollywood set that had long been part of O'Dell's life. An anecdote will provide a glimpse into the sort of lifestyle they led. The O'Dells threw a splashy party that required moving much of their furniture to a warehouse to make room for the burgeoning guest list. During the party, the warehouse went up in flames, destroying all their furniture. It may be that O'Dell's gregarious habits inhibited his writing output, or, perhaps just as likely, he was naturally undisciplined. His longtime friend and editor Austin Olney, when asked whether O'Dell had any weaknesses as a writer, responded without hesitation, "Laziness."[10] At the very least, O'Dell seems to have been easily tempted away from the typewriter. He certainly had never been prolific. But married life, however erratic it may have been, imposed some stability, for his writing output increased during these years. From 1947 to 1955 he remained as book editor of the *Daily News*. In addition, he collaborated with a prison convict, William Doyle (an alias), to write *Man Alone*, published in 1953. In 1957, *Country of the Sun: Southern California, an Informal Guide* appeared; 1958 saw the publication of another adult historical novel, *The Sea Is Red*. These books met with limited success, and it was not until 1960, when he was 62 years old, that his literary star finally rose with the publication of *Island of the Blue Dolphins*.

Like so many other eminent children's authors, O'Dell did not set out to write a book for children. He had a story he wanted to tell and he told it in the best way he knew how. Thus, at an age when most of his contemporaries were contemplating retirement, he entered the most productive and rewarding years of his life. Between 1960 and his death in 1989 he published more than 25 books, most of them historical fiction for young readers.

He and his first wife separated in 1966 and ultimately divorced. It was also during the mid-1960s that he met his second wife, Elizabeth Hall.[11] His life with Hall proved much more conducive to writing than had his often exasperating years with his first wife, who apparently little understood or appreciated her husband's talent. Hall, on the other hand, was an intellectual soul mate for O'Dell. Originally a librarian, with a background in psychology, Hall became O'Dell's confidante and sounding board for his literary ideas. In turn, he encouraged her to write and they proved a mutually beneficial team. O'Dell had no children of his own, but he treated Hall's two children by her previous marriage as his own. In addition to their literary interests, O'Dell and Hall shared a love of the sea and together spent a great deal of time sailing. They traveled extensively, particularly when O'Dell was researching a book. All in all, it was an extraordinarily happy relationship.

Once O'Dell discovered his niche in children's historical fiction, he found it easier to write with a routine, and this undoubtedly contributed to his vastly expanded output during the last three decades of his life. When he was working on a book, O'Dell typically refused all social and speaking engagements, becoming a virtual hermit. Writing historical fiction required a fair amount of research, and he read a great deal. Initially, he composed at a typewriter, but once he gave up cigarettes, he found he had to give up the typewriter as well, so close was its association for him with smoking. After that he wrote out all his books in longhand, often using yellow legal pads and a black pen. He preferred to rise early in the morning, sometimes as early as 5:00 A.M., and write until about noon. His wife would then type what he wrote so he could review it later and make revisions. He never employed a secretary. Once or twice a week the couple would go out to lunch where O'Dell would share his ideas with his wife and discuss his progress, plot development, character motivation, and other aspects of his current project.

In 1975, Elizabeth Hall became managing editor of *Psychology Today,* a job that required her to move East. Since he could do his writing anywhere, O'Dell happily obliged his wife, and they left the West that had been his lifelong home to settle in Westchester County, New York. O'Dell adapted well to his new surroundings. He purchased a home on a secluded lake, furnished it in California style, and resumed his writing. In fact, Westchester County gave him the inspiration for a new historical novel, *Sarah Bishop,* the story of a local eccentric of the late eighteenth–early nineteenth centuries. Perhaps O'Dell's ready adjustment to his new environment can be attributed in part to his incurable wanderlust. He once said, "I love to travel. Travel to me is more important than anything."[12] O'Dell's true world was the world of his imagination, the flame of which was kindled by his extensive travels and his reading. He was not one to become sentimentally attached to a piece of ground. The world contained too much fascination for him to confine himself by geographical attachments. Although he was extremely sensitive, his mind was too lively, too inquisitive to be burdened with sentimentality. He lived happily in New York for the rest of his life.

By the time he reached his eighties, O'Dell had become a venerated figure in children's literature. In 1984, to help reward the profession that had so honored him and to encourage the writing of historical fiction, he established the Scott O'Dell Award for Historical Fiction. The winning book must be set in the Western Hemisphere and must have been published in English. The award carries a prize of $5,000 and is administered and presented annually by the *Bulletin of the Center for Children's Books* to a distinguished work of historical fiction for young readers. (O'Dell himself was even awarded the prize in 1987 for *Streams to the River, River to the Sea.*) The award continues to carry considerable prestige.

One of O'Dell's great joys was interacting with his young readers. He loved visiting schools and reading and responding to his mail from children. He found their honesty and enthusiasm refreshing. After having written for adult audiences for more than half his life, he discovered that he preferred to write for young children because he believed he could more likely have an impact on them. O'Dell was unapologetically a moralist. He once claimed that he was influenced in his writing by two people: an unnamed ancestor who was an itinerant preacher in the Cumberland Gap and Albert Schweitzer, "who preached reverence for all life."[13] From these two he acquired a strong ethical sense that permeated virtually everything he wrote. O'Dell was not, however, a religious man; he cared little, especially, for institutionalized religion. For a long time, he had admired Father Junípero Serra, the eighteenth-century founder of southern California missions. But when O'Dell suspected that Serra's actions were deliberately calculated to procure a sainthood for himself, he lost all interest in him. On the other hand, he had a life-long admiration for Saint Francis of Assisi, perhaps because of the saint's genuine disdain for the institutional trappings of the church as well as his devotion to all things living. It is with this unclouded ethical sense that O'Dell imbued his books, and this constitutes no small part of his appeal for young readers.

Through the 1970s and 1980s O'Dell wrote tirelessly, producing a book a year until his death from prostate cancer on 15 October 1989. At his death, he had two works in progress, both of which were completed, at his request, by his widow. The first, *Thunder Rolling in the Mountains,* a story of Chief Joseph of the Nez Percé, was nearer completion and was published three years after his death. The second, *Venus among the Fishes,* was largely a concept, and most of that work, published in 1995, must be attributed to Elizabeth Hall.

Scott O'Dell's memorial service was held at the Mid-Manhattan Library. Madeleine L'Engle, a longtime friend and a Newbery Award winner herself, was one of the eulogists. On 19 February 1990, his ashes were scattered over the Pacific, off the coast of La Jolla, California—so at the end he fittingly came to rest in the bosom of his lifelong love and inspiration, the sea. There is a charming story that the boat carrying the mourners was accompanied, on its return to port at Mission Bay, by an honor guard of playful, leaping dolphins. If the story is not true, it surely ought to be.

Scott O'Dell, who came to children's books relatively late in life, and almost unawares, left an indelible mark on the field. In addition to the Newbery Medal, the three Newbery Honor books, and the Hans Christian Andersen Medal, O'Dell received numerous other honors for his works—the University of Southern Mississippi Award, the Catholic Library Association Regina Medal, and the OMAR Award, to name but a few. The majority of O'Dell's books for young readers are still in print, and he remains one of the most popular writers of historical fiction for children. One critic summarizes O'Dell's achievement as follows: "His rank as one of the foremost historical novelists is attested to by the number of prestigious awards he has won, by the thousands and thousands of young readers he has claimed since the publication of *Island of the Blue Dolphins* in 1960, and by the critical acclaim he has received for several of his books."[14] Another says, "His writings have and will stand the test of time, because his message is so potent and accurate that it speaks to all generations."[15] O'Dell's close friends, editor Austin Olney and Olney's wife, Marcia Legru, described him as gallant and courtly, a man with a grand style.[16] He imbued his characters with this same gallantry and style. In the final analysis, it is O'Dell himself who perhaps best identified the enduring quality of his writings: "With all my books, I've tried to dramatize the importance of the dignity of the human spirit" ("Dignity," 185).

Chapter Two

The Writer's Beginnings: Works for Adults

Writing is hard work, harder than digging a ditch, and it requires patience.

—O'Dell, quoted in *Something about the Author* (1990)

O'Dell's first published book appeared in 1924, a work titled *Representative Photoplays Analyzed* and intended for aspiring writers. During the early 1920s, O'Dell was employed by the Palmer Institute in Los Angeles as a mail-order instructor of photoplay writing. *Representative Photoplays* is a lengthy work of nearly 500 pages, providing synopses of some 105 photoplays—we would call them screenplays today. O'Dell analyzes the photoplays so that readers, in the words of editor and publisher Frederick Palmer, "may check [their] material against the product of some of the world's most successful photoplaywrights."[1] The research and writing of the book must have been an exhaustive effort, perhaps made more pleasurable by O'Dell's early love of the cinema. As a literary contribution, however, it remains a curiosity, of interest mainly to film historians for its assessments of such early silent versions as *Alice Adams, The Sea Wolf, The Prisoner of Zenda,* and *The Ten Commandments* (Cecil B. DeMille's first effort at that story, which would be followed many decades later with his more famous extravaganza starring Charlton Heston as Moses). Just a few years after the book's publication, talkies appeared and quickly made the silent films (and O'Dell's book) fairly obsolete. O'Dell was surely under no illusion that this was a significant creative work; however, in it he displays a keenly critical eye, one that he would use in his years as a book reviewer. It is also quite likely that this exercise honed his sense of story line. And we find in his later works an almost cinematic quality, with his attention to setting, his insistence on lively action and colorful characters, and his aversion to both lengthy exposition and philosophical musings. Although O'Dell eventually lost interest in film—in his later years he rarely attended the cinema—its influence persisted.

As a novelist, O'Dell had an unusually lengthy germination period. His first published novel would not appear until he was in his thirties, and more than a dozen years would pass before his second. His early novels were adventure romances intended for adults, although not entirely inappropriate for adolescent readers, and it is easy to see how he was able to make the transition to writing for young people. A look at his works for adults will reveal the lifelong interests that would become the chief preoccupations of his successful juvenile fiction.

Woman of Spain: A Story of Old California

Woman of Spain, subtitled *A Story of Old California,* was published in 1934 and reflects O'Dell's passion for the Spanish history of California, his love of the sea, and his fondness for strong female protagonists. Spanning a two-year period from about 1819 to 1821, the story follows the adventures of Marta Salazar, the younger of two daughters of a family of Spanish immigrants journeying to the San Francisco Bay area, where they have received a land grant from the Spanish king. Marta's mother, Luisa, is a strong-willed, hardworking woman who holds the family together. Her father, Sebastian, is a worthless reprobate, whose affair with a married woman was the cause of their abruptly leaving their home in Spain. Her older sister, Ysabel, Sebastian's favorite, is looking for the easy life and lacks the drive and ambition that characterize Marta.

The family's land is not far from the Mission Dolores, whose majordomo is an American named Matt Reider. An effective leader who has brought a measure of prosperity to the faltering mission, he is also greedy and unscrupulous and is at odds with Lieutenant Bastierra, commander of the presidio, over landownership on the peninsula. Matt sees the arrival of the Salazars as a threat to his plans to control the land on the peninsula, and he schemes to drive them off, although they have the protection of the kindly Bastierra. The final principal character is a seaman named Jared Wyeth, a native of Salem, Massachusetts. He is first mate on the trading vessel *China Bride,* bringing goods from the Orient in exchange for hides and other merchandise. Jared is quickly intrigued with Marta for her hard-driving bargains and strength of character as well as her beauty. He gives her a costly shawl (one intended, in fact, for his fiancée in New England), and she insists that she will repay him in hides when he returns. Shortly after, Marta's mother, worn down by the incessant, backbreaking work on the ranch, sickens and dies. Sebastian is ready to return the grant to the king and head for what he believes to be a softer life further south in Monterey, a plan equally agreeable to Ysabel. However, Marta feels an obligation to her mother and refuses to leave. Her trump card is her threat to expose Sebastian's sordid past, and he grudgingly succumbs to her will, which is evidently as strong as her mother's.

Marta gets little help from her father and sister in maintaining the ranch, and Father Torme from the mission encourages her to stay on the land and to take Matt as her husband and helpmeet. Although Marta confesses to strong feelings for Jared, she accepts Matt's courtship. She cannot be sure that Jared will ever return, and she desperately needs help on the land. In the meantime, Lieutenant Bastierra marries Ysabel, and on the wedding day, the *China Bride* returns to the harbor—but without Jared. Dejected and in a moment of great vulnerability, Marta accepts Matt's marriage proposal. After their betrothal, Matt becomes more oppressive than ever, and Marta soon realizes her mistake.

Jared does return, however; this time on his own ship, aptly named the *Señorita*. The growing conflict between the United States and Spain over territorial rights in the West has made Jared's position precarious, and he must sail or risk confiscation of his ship. A complex series of events culminates in Marta's jilting Matt on their wedding day so that she may warn Jared that his ship risks being seized and that he must sail immediately. Jared confesses his love for her and begs her to come with him, but she cannot leave the land, and so they part.

Marta is put on trial for conspiring with a Yankee ship against the law, the penalty for which would be the revocation of her land grant. Ironically, it is Matt who comes to her rescue, and, although grateful that her land has been spared, Marta continues to reject Matt, which for him is the final straw. He engineers a stampede of wild horses through her land to wreak havoc, but in the process, he is maimed for life— apparently just retribution for his avarice and cruelty. Marta is pregnant with Jared's child—which will be a surprise to many readers, the seduction scene having been so innocuously handled. Her father, in one final act of brutality, beats her for disgracing him and leaves. It is Matt, a ruined man, who points out to Marta that Jared's ship has returned, and she runs to meet it. But her time to deliver approaches, and she returns to her home just in time to find Jared waiting for her.

Woman of Spain is a well-told story, reasonably fast-paced, if somewhat predictable and occasionally melodramatic. As would be true of his entire writing career, character development is not O'Dell's strong suit.

He prefers to lavish his talent on an exciting plot and evocative setting. His stories are as much about the land he loves as about the people who live on it. In *Woman of Spain,* we see his love of old California, especially its history, its Spanish culture. We see also his fondness of the sea. An avid sailor, he knew that Jared would never be able to give up the sailor's life for farming, as Marta realizes as she and Jared embrace on the final page of the book:

> His gaze was turned to the sea. In an instant revelation she knew upon what it rested and the sacrifice she would be forced to make. To his first love she had relinquished him before, on the headland and beside the fire. The time would soon come for her to give him back again, for as long as the ship lived she would possess only a part of him, that part which the sea could not claim. Until then he was hers and she was happy.[2]

First novels often fall prey to a weighty, pretentious style, and O'Dell, whose crisp, sparse prose was to become his hallmark, does occasionally succumb to the temptation of poetic descriptions:

> The *China Bride* rose slowly to the long green waves and slowly descended. The morning sun flashed on her bright copper sheathing and the yellow planking of her deck. Through valleys of water ribbed with foam, her black prow slid with a prolonged and gentle hiss. Her canvas, bellowing to the fresh wind, bore her onwards towards the Bay of Saint Francis. (*Woman,* 59)

In the preceding passage we can feel O'Dell's passion for the sea, its exuberance, its thrilling colors. His love of nature and respect for all living things are evident in passages such as the following:

> The seasons shifted before their time. After a long interval of heavy rains, followed by clear, warm days, a false spring came. In the meadows a few, fragile flowers appeared; the tiny seeds of the redwoods coiled and ripened; from the forest at night, loud on the windy air, was borne the call of mountain lions; hawks, cruising above the fields in mating play, uttered their solitary cries. . . . (*Woman,* 285)

O'Dell even brings the wildlife of the region into unwitting roles as characters in his story:

> The moon, breasting a tide of wind-driven fog, rose above the ridge, and in the soft whiteness that poured down through the trees, far ahead

where the trail opened out into the clearing, the walls of the house showed, the red blur of candlelight, the reflection of evening fire on grass and leaf. A wolf bitch in the brush a dozen paces away, who had followed the train since dusk, stopped and watched it pass with green-glowing eyes. (*Woman,* 117)

Woman of Spain differs in narrative technique from most other O'Dell novels in that it is told from the point of view of an omniscient narrator. This allows O'Dell to draw certain parallels in his story. For example, in one chapter we see Jared pitying all those "earth-bound people . . . who didn't follow the sea" (*Woman,* 63), and in the succeeding chapter we see Marta wondering "how men could live their lives upon the sea, coming from strange places and returning, always in danger, never knowing a true home" (*Woman,* 65). Thus the fundamental differences in their characters are delineated, differences that they must ultimately face as they realize their love for one another. One wonders why O'Dell abandoned the omniscient narrative in his later works, particularly because the first-person narrator he came to favor does not always suit his tales of high adventure. He perhaps sensed his penchant for an overwrought exposition and relied on the first-person storyteller to diminish this intrusiveness. However, in *Woman of Spain,* he clearly demonstrates his facility with an alternative narrative style.

Another noteworthy feature of *Woman of Spain* is O'Dell's use of the strong female protagonist. Marta is the forebear of Karana, Zia, Carlota, Lucinda, Alexandra, and other O'Dell heroines who must fight their own battles with little help from anyone, man or woman, and who prefer to meet life on their own terms. These women are fearless, both physically and emotionally strong, independent, and determined. They have a powerful sense of their own past, of their historical roots, and that is partly what gives them their strength of character. Theirs is a commitment to a way of life as much as to their own survival.

Finally, *Woman of Spain* illustrates O'Dell's deep sense of history, his respect for the arduous task of his pioneering predecessors. O'Dell's native southern California is rich in Spanish heritage, and he was profoundly influenced by the culture. Nearly half of his novels deal with Spanish-American culture in one way or another—and most of those with history. *Woman of Spain,* unlike many of his later works, keeps the focus on the Spaniards and Americans of European ancestry. The native Indians play virtually no role in the story. They live and work at the mission, and we hear occasional stories of marauding tribes, but none are given form as individual characters. This omission would be corrected in several later books devoted entirely to Native Americans.

Probably because of its predictability, its sometimes rambling structure, and its failure to provide truly engaging characters, *Woman of Spain* was never reprinted and is little read today. But it is important in our study of O'Dell as indicative of the various seeds of thought that would come to fruition in his best books for young readers.

Hill of the Hawk

Hill of the Hawk did not appear until 1947, some 13 years after *Woman of Spain,* although O'Dell began the book prior to the Second World War. Once again, the author turns to the early history of California—this time to the period of the Mexican War, 1846 to 1848. It is the story of Grady Dunavant, an American trader and sometime warrior, and a proud and passionate woman of an old Spanish family, Luz Zubaran, who bears a strong resemblance to Marta Salazar. Luz's father, Don Saturnino, owns the Hill of the Hawk, a large ranch east of the pueblo of Los Angeles, and he hates the Americans, or, as he contemptuously calls them, the gringos. Grady is a former U.S. Army lieutenant of impeccable record, now engaged in trade between Los Angeles and the American cities to the east. He possesses all the expected heroic attributes— good looks, strength and physical prowess, worldliness, and soft-spoken charm. Grady and Luz are attracted to each other from the first time they meet, although at the time they both believe their lives to be headed in dramatically different directions.

At the novel's opening, Grady is on his way to Los Angeles to marry pretty Camilla Howland, the daughter of Kate Howland, one of the pueblo's most successful entrepreneurs. However, to his dismay, Grady discovers that she is already betrothed to an Englishman (who was, in fact, one of Grady's fellow travelers on his pack train). The insult is doubly painful because of the strained relations between the United States and Great Britain, the latter having made noises about supporting the Mexicans in the United States–Mexican dispute. O'Dell's inclusion of both historical events and historical personages makes this work a classic example of the historical novel. Grady reaches Los Angeles at a time when the United States is rattling its sabers the loudest, and the corrupt Mexican government, which is understandably less than genial to the

Americans in California, is tightening its reins. Grady, after being jilted by Camilla, accepts an offer to help lead a rebellion, and he sets off for San Diego to round up troops. On the way he encounters Luz Zubaran once again, and the magnetism between them is apparent—to everyone except them. Luz, very much like her father, professes hatred for the Americans. Grady, despite his mission for his country, seems more opportunistic than patriotic—he flatly admits that he does not understand manifest destiny—and his goal is at times more personal than altruistic. Fraser, the Englishman who won Camilla's hand, and the evil Curel, a faithless soldier from Grady's past, are both aiding the Mexicans—enough reason for Grady to take up arms against them. By a clever ruse, Grady manages to have Fraser and Curel shipped to the Sandwich Islands, and he heads back to Los Angeles where the crisis is heating up.

Meanwhile, Luz, who has heretofore dressed in rather functional rancher's clothing, goes to Los Angeles and purchases a dress, a sure sign that she is weakening, admitting to herself that she is in love with Grady. Shortly after, Luz arranges to meet Grady, ostensibly to warn him that her brother is hunting him, but, in fact, she confesses her love for him and they consummate their love—a scene that O'Dell handles with particular delicacy; he never wrote a lascivious passage in his life. Now Grady realizes that he, too, loves her. Soon after, Grady is seriously wounded by Luz's brother and is brought by Luz to the Hill of the Hawk, an act that incurs the considerable wrath of Saturnino, who viciously beats his daughter. Luz and Grady are saved only through the indomitable will of Carlota de Zubaran, Saturnino's aged mother and one of the more delightful characters in the novel. A woman of fierce temperament, she is the only person whom Saturnino fears. O'Dell describes her habit of using one of her young servants as a footstool, resting her feet on his back. He will use this same image again in *Carlota,* a book for children also on the subject of the Mexican War and with many striking similarities. Carlota de Zubaran is a pragmatist who "like her husband before her . . . believed that the wisest policy was to do nothing which would incite reprisals. If the Americans took over California, their government could be no worse than that of the Mexicans."[3] After the assault by Luz's brother, Grady is taken to Los Angeles and imprisoned along with other Americans, including Kate Howland. Carlota and Luz go to Los Angeles to try to rescue Grady, but their efforts are thwarted by Yris Llorente, a beautiful woman with a past who has long held a torch for Grady. When he rejects her advances, he earns her enmity, and she manipulates events to make it appear that Luz has abandoned Grady in his time of need.

Eventually, the Americans do win, of course. Among other incidents, O'Dell relates the true story of a famous ride from Los Angeles to San Francisco in record time by a young man named Juan Flaco—an interesting tale, but of scant relevance to the plot. Once the Americans, with their superior force, take over Los Angeles, they foolishly impose a repressive regime, which in time incites an insurrection. O'Dell is nothing if not evenhanded in his treatment of the politics. In the meantime, Grady buys the Hill of the Hawk, which is among the spoils of war, from Kate Howland, Don Saturnino's creditor. He had admired the ranch, but we suspect his motives are more out of revenge against Luz, who he believes betrayed him. It is Carlota who again intervenes. She refuses to leave her home, and Grady discovers he is helpless to remove her. Carlota continues to act as if she is the mistress of the Hill of the Hawk, and Grady shrugs his shoulders and acquiesces. Her plan is, of course, to bring Grady and Luz back together—and she succeeds: she always succeeds.

When the Spaniards retake Los Angeles, the ranch reverts to Don Saturnino. But Grady and Luz meet secretly, taking refuge in an abandoned cabin. Grady rounds up a priest who marries them. Shortly after, Don Saturnino is clawed to death by his pet eagle—so violent a man is not permitted the honor of dying in battle. O'Dell describes the events surrounding the arrival of the Army of the West under General Stephen W. Kearny and Kit Carson—a story he will again recount in *Carlota*—and the Americans finally win the war. The book closes with Grady and Luz reinstalled at the Hill of the Hawk—and with Luz pregnant.

This brief summary cannot begin to suggest the rich detail of the work. O'Dell captures much of the complexity of the political climate of California in the 1840s. Some Californians supported the Mexican government, others supported the Americans, a few supported the British, and many had no strong loyalties so long as they were left alone. We sense the frustration felt by the people when one inept government is replaced by another. O'Dell portrays the mingling of the races in the Old West and adamantly refuses to stereotype peoples. Americans, Mexicans, and Indians all intermarry, and the good and the wicked people are identified not by their race or nationality but by their character. The most interesting characters—as is often the case with O'Dell— are women. Luz de Zubaran, her grandmother, Carlota, the siren Yris

Llorente, the shrewd businesswoman Kate Howland—all are wise, determined, and strong of heart. This book was written long before either the feminist or the civil rights movements, yet O'Dell demonstrates profound sensitivity to both feminist and racial causes (in this case, Native American and Hispanic—no African Americans appear in this book, but Curel is a described as a Creole).

O'Dell the historical novelist is keenly tuned in to details of daily life that give his story and its setting verisimilitude. He describes the laundry day for a large ranch household (a day that might arrive only once every three months). He describes the making of the food, the supervision of the household, the arranging of a fandango, that most spectacular of social gatherings. His geography is keen, as we might expect from a native of the area, and his description of the landscape is clearly that of someone who has ridden the hills and valleys and surveyed the coast. In one of his few historical slips, O'Dell twice refers to the British "king," even though in the 1840s Queen Victoria was securely on the throne.

Hill of the Hawk did not remain long in print, and it received rather scant critical notice. This is perhaps because the book lacks a clearly identifiable audience. Readers interested in the romance between Grady and Luz will require more passion and less historical detail. Readers interested in the adventure of the Old West will wish for less of the minutiae of daily living. Readers interested in character will wish for characters, particularly antagonists, less shallow and more engaging. Don Saturnino, the villain, has little depth. Even Grady remains a shadowy figure, handsome and decent, but in many respects the stereotypical Western hero—a strong-minded individual, silent and brooding, and free of attachments. However, the book is generally well paced, a quality aided by O'Dell's use of the omniscient narrator and his movement among a variety of settings—from the pueblo of Los Angeles to the ranches to the harbor at San Diego. This would be O'Dell's last use of the omniscient narrator, even though he would write several books that could have greatly benefited from that point of view. The story has an epic sweep to it, cataloging a political and social upheaval. It is the story of a people at war and of the death of one way of life and the birth of another. Such a story requires larger-than-life figures to carry it through. In the final estimate, Grady and Luz are too mundane to shoulder that burden; events too often direct their lives and not the other way around as we expect from heroes. Grady and Luz are more like the people next door—they pique our curiosity, but do not fire our passion.

Man Alone

O'Dell's next published book was not his own, but rather one he edited and polished. *Man Alone* (1953) is a real-life narrative about a man's 20 years in prison for murder. The author's real name and that of the prison are not divulged. He goes by the name William Doyle, and the prison is called McGraw. Doyle's nephew knew O'Dell, which was how Doyle came to him for help in getting his memoirs published. He gave O'Dell a rambling manuscript of some 300,000 words, which was, in O'Dell's words, "full of repetitions and irrelevancies."[4] But it was also a gripping account that he could not lay down. O'Dell was extremely modest when assessing his part of this joint venture. But the work was trimmed to about one-fourth of its original length largely due to O'Dell's advice. In some cases, where O'Dell recommended changes, Doyle steadfastly refused, insisting that he wanted events to be reported as they actually had happened. Doyle clearly intended his work as a social message: "Yes, prison is a hellish place. If my story deters some other young man from taking the first step that leads there, it will have fulfilled its purpose, and doubly so if it serves in some small way to hasten prison reform in those places—and there are many—where reform is needed" (*Man,* foreword).

It is impossible to assess the extent of O'Dell's impact on the final product, and we are perhaps wisest to accept his own disclaimer in the foreword. Briefly, the book recounts the prison experience of a convicted murderer who maintained his innocence his whole life. His descriptions of prison life in the 1930s and 1940s are appalling. In great detail he depicts the unsanitary conditions, the unsavory food, the abusive treatment from the prison guards. The book includes some fine drama: There is an attempted prison break, during which Doyle personally saves several men's lives, and after which he refuses to turn state's evidence even though it would mean a pardon. There are his experiences in the "hole"—solitary confinement where he once spent 19 days naked in the damp, cold dark. He lost 18 pounds and spent two months in the hospital to recover. There is his secret visit to the death chamber, and the rare tender moment when he describes the prisoners adopting and caring for stray animals—until the creatures are brutally killed by insensitive guards. And there is a second attempted prison break, which results in the death of the warden. Doyle was eventually paroled by an enlightened parole board who acknowledged his valor in saving lives during the first attempted break. Although he maintained his innocence, Doyle refused to violate the principle of "honor" among prisoners, never giving in to the temptation to betray his fellow prisoners in return for favors or even parole.

In the course of this moving and insightful narrative, Doyle, himself, attains a certain dignity as he endures the wretched existence to which he is condemned. O'Dell had a deep sense of human dignity shining through in the worst of circumstances, and it is perhaps in this quality of *Man Alone* that we can see his most profound influence. He would never undertake another venture such as this, for in a short time his own reputation would be made, but the result of this collaboration, its rough edges aside, is a work not easily forgotten.

The Sea Is Red

For his next book, O'Dell returned to historical fiction, his first love. *The Sea Is Red* would be his last novel for adults, although, as we will see, O'Dell had no idea of that at the time. O'Dell chose a subject that he was to resurrect later in a book for young readers, *The 290*—that of the legendary Confederate ship the *Alabama*. *The Sea Is Red* appeared in 1957, when O'Dell was nearly 60. It was only his third novel, his writing career up to this point having been by and large journalistic. This time, he turned to the sea as the primary setting, and he also turned to the first-person narrator, a style he apparently found so compatible that he never abandoned it.

Told by Kirk Britt, a young entrepreneur and captain of a trading vessel, the story takes place in the Caribbean during the 1860s. Britt comes from a family of slave dealers, although he himself is horrified by the inhumanity of the practice. At the book's outset, Britt finds himself the unwitting participant in a failed insurrection in Haiti, during which he rescues the powerful and avaricious Don Ruiz Capanegra, a Cuban slave dealer, and his beautiful and mysterious wife, Doña Elise. Britt returns them to their home, a castle in Cuba where he learns of Don Ruiz's plan to return the West Indies to Spanish rule. This curious theme will return once again in a more elaborate version in *The Spanish Smile* and its sequel, *The Castle in the Sea*. In all three cases, the idea suggests a crazed megalomania, and Don Ruiz is, indeed, a fearsome creature, one of the most dastardly of O'Dell's villains. It is Capanegra who is responsible for sending Britt up the Mississippi to New Orleans knowing full well that an ambush by Federal troops awaits. In the attack, Britt loses his ship and his young wife. The losses drive Britt to join the crew of a Confederate warship, the *Sumter,* and a series of adventures follow, including a mutiny resulting in Britt's temporary imprisonment. He soon becomes convinced of Don Ruiz's complicity in his tragedies and vows vengeance against him as well as against the North. A slave trader named Armand Thiot induces Britt to help transport a shipload of slaves, and the experience sickens him. His loyalties are shaken, for although he hates the North for killing his wife, he finds that he has no stomach for slavery. This tension will be with him throughout the story—although, in fact, Britt is not subject to a great deal of profound soul-searching. He then finds himself the virtual prisoner of Don Ruiz, but Doña Elise aids his escape along with a former slave Cicerón, who takes him to a village of runaway slaves, where he learns to detest slavery.

At this point, the story takes a surprising twist, and Britt ends up in Liverpool, where, at Laird's shipyard, the *290,* a ship destined to become the most successful of the Confederate raiders, is nearing completion. Following a series of intrigues (once again involving the ubiquitous Don Ruiz, who turns up in England), Britt joins the crew of the *290,* which is christened *Alabama,* and the famous ship's exploits are recounted. Among the ship's journeys is a visit to a Brazilian prison island where Britt meets Tina Schilling, the daughter of a convicted German forger, and a romance develops, but Britt must soon sail. The *Alabama* meets her fate in Cherbourg Harbor in a battle with the Federal warship *Kearsarge;* Britt, rescued from the wreckage, buys a schooner and heads for Cuba.

In Cuba he discovers a rebellion afoot and joins with the runaway slaves in their attempted siege of Don Ruiz's fortress. In the most dramatic scene of the book, the captured Britt is alone in a room with the mad Don Ruiz, who is about to order a cannon firing on the attacking runaways. He finds himself unable to murder Don Ruiz, however; then, unexpectedly, Doña Elise enters the room, and without a word stabs Don Ruiz to death.

Britt now returns to Haiti, where he quickly rebuilds his fortune and sets out for the Brazilian prison island to renew his courtship of Tina Schilling. Over her father's objections, they escape from the island and marry. The book closes with a picture of Britt, his wife, and daughter living happily in Port-au-Prince. But the sorrows and burdens of his life have not left Britt unscathed. Far off in the hills the drums beat, deceptively dreamlike and peaceful, but he recognizes in them a warning—

"the voice of the Furies—one of the many voices of those implacable barterers for man's happiness which have decreed that Evil is not to be redeemed, but only compounded."[5] This brief summary can only suggest the convolutions of the plot. The story is packed with swashbuckling adventure, although only an incurable romantic could believe the interlude on the Brazilian prison island and Britt's good fortune at finding a beautiful woman there (who happily can speak French, as does Britt). The first-person narrator poses a problem for a story such as this. If the narrator is also the hero, he or she risks coming across as an egoist. The more satisfactory first-person narrator is the observer, in which case the protagonist is another character in the story, whose heroic exploits can be properly (and modestly) celebrated. In *The Sea Is Red,* the author walks gingerly between the two methods. Britt must tell his story without seeming to blow his own horn—but when he is too self-effacing, O'Dell risks losing our interest in his main character. And Britt's shallow characterization is precisely the problem. His first wife is treated as almost an incidental character, included explicitly for the purpose of being killed in the Northern ambush, thus giving impetus to Britt's hatred of the North. We see little of the widower's grief at his wife's death, just as we see little of the lover's passion in his relationship with Tina Schilling. This is not really a book about character, for Britt remains largely one-dimensional in the face of so many dire consequences—loss of fortune, friends, family, wife. He is more of an observer of the dramatic events surrounding him, rather than an active participant. Britt is the ostensible hero of a romance-adventure-war story in which he kills no one and the only recorded kiss is one that "tasted of mangoes" (*Sea,* 214). Indeed, in the most dramatic moment of the book, when Doña Elise stabs her wicked husband, Britt can only watch in paralyzed amazement.

In *The Sea Is Red,* it is tempting to see a writer of young people's fiction struggling to emerge. O'Dell is clearly not interested in love stories, nor is he much interested in writing about the human response to grief. This is not to say that these topics are not of interest to young readers, but they are not burning issues for most youthful audiences. O'Dell is interested in the strength of the human spirit, in the assertion of the individual against an antagonistic environment. He is interested in the means of survival against overwhelming odds; he is interested in justice, the triumph of good over evil. O'Dell imbued his fiction, from the very beginning, with a strong moral purpose. Britt, in one of his more philosophical moments, characterizes Don Ruiz:

He was a Spaniard, and the history of his family, like that of all the
Spaniards who had come to the Indies for glory and gold, was a story of
unbridled rapacity existing side by side with the purest idealism, of unex-
ampled bravery and abject cowardice. They had conquered the islands
against great odds, a handful of men against thousands, perished in its
swamps, endured heat and cold, starvation and fever. They had established towns and modeled them after their homes in Spain, with law and
life's amenities. They had brought the Cross, but with it, the whip. The
native Arawaks, once given the blessings of religion, were worked to
death on their plantations, shipped to Mexico to die in the deep shafts of
their silver mines, decimated almost to a man. (*Sea,* 37–38)

In this passage we find the genesis of several themes that O'Dell would
flesh out in his books for young people: the imposition of European culture on the native cultures of the New World, the inhumane treatment
of Native Americans, the sin of greed, the horror of slavery. He was
poised to embark—unawares—on a new direction in his career.

Conclusion

Country of the Sun: Southern California, An Informal History and Guide was
published the same year as *The Sea Is Red,* 1957. The subtitle aptly
describes the book's contents—historical anecdotes depicting the colorful past of O'Dell's native California. The book contains a wealth of
information, ranging from the pronunciation of Spanish words to descriptions of local festivals. It is both a resource of obscure information
and a storehouse of delightful reading, although now rather dated.

As we can see, the first six decades of O'Dell's life saw little of promise
spring from his pen. O'Dell's apprenticeship was lengthy, his early success sporadic, and it must have seemed to him at times that his career as
a writer was destined to wither on the vine. But his years of perseverance
and steady preparation were about to pay off, for just ahead lay his finest
work. With one or two exceptions, O'Dell's subsequent books would be
for children. (*The Cruise of the Arctic Star,* a book for all ages, will be discussed in chapter 5. In 1967, he helped write the text for *The Psychology
of Children's Art* by Rhoda Kellogg; he was not, however, responsible for
the content.) The situations and themes of O'Dell's adult works foreshadow his later interests, and in them we can see the seeds of his later
success.

Chapter Three
Island of the Blue Dolphins

The human heart, lonely and in need of love, is a vessel which needs replenishing.
—O'Dell, quoted in *Something about the Author* (1990)

Scott O'Dell did not intend to write a children's book when he wrote *Island of the Blue Dolphins.* He was genuinely surprised when it was suggested to him that it belonged on the juvenile list. He once said,

> I didn't know what young people were reading and I didn't consider [*Island of the Blue Dolphins*] a children's book, necessarily. [It] was a protest against the hunters who came into our mountains and killed everything that crept or walked or flew.
>
> I sent the story to my agents. They sent it back to me by return mail, saying that if I was serious about the story I should change the girl to a boy, because girls were only interested in romance and such. This seemed silly to me. So I picked up the story, went to New York City, and gave it to my editor, who accepted it the next day. When it won the Newbery Medal, I was launched into writing for children and young adults. (Hopkins, 133–34)

O'Dell never returned to writing adult novels. This was the beginning of virtually a new career for O'Dell. He was finally reaping the rewards of his long years of apprenticeship. Then came an even greater surprise—*Island of the Blue Dolphins* was awarded the Newbery Medal for the most distinguished contribution to children's books in America. Even though O'Dell was a seasoned writer, for a first-time children's author to win the Newbery Medal is an astonishing feat. It was the beginning of a brilliant decade of one award-winning book after another.

Island of the Blue Dolphins would win numerous other awards, both national and international, including the German Juvenile International Award, the Nene Award, the OMAR Award, the Rupert Hughes Award, the Southern California Council on Literature for Children and

Young People Notable Book Award, and the Hans Christian Andersen Award of Merit. The book appears on most lists of modern classics and ranks with the finest American fiction for young people written in the last half of the twentieth century.

The Origin of the Story

Scott O'Dell wrote that *Island of the Blue Dolphins* "began in anger, anger at the hunters who invade the mountains where I live and who slaughter everything that creeps or walks or flies. This anger was also directed at myself, at the young man of many years ago, who thoughtlessly committed the same crimes against nature."[1] O'Dell wrote his novel because he thought that it would reach a larger audience than the letter to the editor he originally planned to write. O'Dell rather modestly described *Island of the Blue Dolphins* as a book "about a girl who kills animals and then learns reverence for all life" (Roop, 751). He could not have anticipated that the work would forever alter the course of his life. After *Island of the Blue Dolphins,* O'Dell would discover that his passion for history and his desire to reach young people with his messages of determination, self-reliance, and humanitarianism provided him with a wellspring of ideas that kept him occupied right up to his death.

As early as the 1920s, O'Dell learned the true story of the "Lost Woman of San Nicolas." From the few facts known about her, he would weave an engaging survival story recounting the 18 years she spent alone on the island. San Nicolas is one of the smallest of the channel islands off the shore of Los Angeles, and it is now uninhabited. But in the early nineteenth century, a small tribe of indigenous people occupied its desolate landscape. The woman was left on the island in 1835 when the rest of the inhabitants were removed by the Americans to the mainland. Reportedly, she jumped from the ship into the sea and swam back to her home, efforts to restrain her having failed. It was not until 1853 that she was discovered again and then removed to Santa Barbara Mission, where little could be learned from her because her own people, in a subsequent tragedy, had not survived and no one else spoke her language. A Father Gonzales at the mission learned that she had a brother who was killed by wild dogs on the island. And she was discovered wearing a skirt of green cormorant feathers, which, according to O'Dell, was sent to Rome. From these bits of information, O'Dell constructed his story of courage, loneliness, and the need for love and understanding in the world.

The Narrative

The story of *Island of the Blue Dolphins* is a straightforward narrative told by Karana, the daughter of the chieftain in the village of Ghalas-at. Her people are a small and impoverished tribe, eking out a living on a barren island, its only significant resource being the sea otters coveted by the Aleuts who arrive in their sailing vessel (captained by a Russian) at the book's opening. Karana's father makes a deal with the Aleuts, bargaining for half the otter pelts they acquire. These pelts Karana's people will then exchange with the Aleuts for beads and other trinkets. The natives of Ghalas-at are therefore condoning the slaughter of animals for mere material gain and display no special ecological sensitivity. In fact, the chieftain laughs at his daughter's "foolishness" when she expresses a concern that the Aleuts might slay all the sea otters. This exchange foreshadows one of the book's principal themes, the importance of humanity's respect for animals.

Several other important aspects of the Aleuts' visit should be noted. First, Karana hears word of a girl accompanying the Aleuts. This is Tutok, who will reappear several years later and form a friendship with Karana. Second, several of the Aleuts' dogs join the wild pack on the island. One of these dogs eventually becomes Rontu, Karana's closest companion on the island during her solitude. Third, Karana has misgivings when her father readily gives his secret name to Captain Orlov, the Russian leader of the Aleut expedition. Karana later becomes certain that this revelation robbed him of his power and contributed to his defeat and death. Years later, Karana will reveal her secret name to Tutok, a sure sign of her trust.

On a less metaphysical level, Karana's father angers the Aleuts in several ways—he drives a hard bargain regarding the otter pelts, and he refuses to share a catch of fish with the hungry Aleuts, preferring to feed his own people first. The built-up antagonism results in a bloody battle between the Aleuts and the people of Ghalas-at, and when it is over, not only Karana's father but most of the young men of the tribe lie dead, and the survivors find it impossible to rebuild their lives with their decimated numbers. The new chief, Kimki, is an elderly man who sees the only hope in his sailing east to the mainland to search for a place to resettle. Kimki's mission to the mainland is successful, and a white man's ship arrives to take the tribe off the island. But as the ship is ready to leave the harbor, Karana's younger brother, Ramo, returns to the village to retrieve his fishing spear. Refusing to leave her brother behind,

Karana jumps overboard, and the ship departs, leaving them stranded on the island—in this way O'Dell invents the pieces missing from the historical account.

Almost immediately, Ramo, who is boastful and immature, disappears, and Karana soon finds his lifeless body surrounded by the pack of wild dogs that roam the island. Thus the scene is set for O'Dell's survival story, unusual for its time because its protagonist is female and a member of a native tribe. Our immediate interest is in how she will overcome the hardships of life on the island and how she might, if ever, be rescued.

After her brother's death, Karana is desolate with grief and remains in the village eating what remains of the store of abalones. But in time, she realizes that she must leave it forever: "I had never noticed before how silent the village was. Fog crept in and out of the empty huts. It made shapes as it drifted and they reminded me of all the people who were dead and those who were gone. The noise of the surf seemed to be their voices speaking."[2] Karana builds a fire and burns the village so that only ashes remain. This drastic step is necessary if she is to move forward and prepare for her own survival. She must erase the haunting memories and free herself to start life anew. Karana also knows that to defend herself against the wild dogs, she will need weapons. At Ramo's death she had vowed that she would "kill the wild dogs in the cave. I would kill all of them" (*Island*, 48). However, because tribal custom has forbidden women access to weapons, she knows neither how to make them nor how to use them, and, perhaps more important, she must struggle with her conscience to overcome the taboo. Karana must do some deep soul-searching:

> Would the four winds blow in from the four directions of the world and smother me as I made the weapons? Or would the earth tremble, as many said, and bury me beneath its falling rocks? Or, as others said, would the sea rise over the island in a terrible flood? Would the weapons break in my hands at the moment when my life was in danger, which is what my father had said? (*Island*, 54)

For two days and three nights she ponders the question, and when the wild dogs return, her resolve is firm: "I made up my mind that no matter what befell me I would make the weapons" (*Island*, 54). And so Karana, out of necessity, further unburdens herself of the past, a visible sign of her growing self-reliance.

After the passage of two winters and an aborted attempt to reach the mainland in a canoe, Karana decides to build a permanent shelter on the island. The details of these efforts are standard fare for survival fiction, as are the details strewn throughout the book of her seeking food and fashioning clothing—skirts from yucca plants and a garment of stunning cormorant feathers. Where O'Dell breaks ranks with earlier writers of survival stories is in his portrayal of the development of Karana's sensibilities as well as her self-reliance. Initially, of course, Karana interacts with her world from the perspective of her tribal mores and customs. She first decides to make a spear using the tooth of a sea elephant and sets out to kill one of the creatures, but she fails and is herself nearly killed in the attempt. She seeks shelter in a cave so that she might nurse herself back to health. Several days later she finds the remains of the old bull sea elephant she had tried to kill—he had been killed by a younger bull—and she finds the tooth she needs for her spear. The processes of nature did for her what she could not do herself.

Her next encounter is with the wild dogs, but this time she wins. Karana kills four of the dogs, but she is fascinated with one particularly large dog that she is sure was one left by the Aleuts. Managing to wound him, she nurses the dog back to health and names him Rontu— "Fox Eyes." Because he has once been tame, redomesticating him is not particularly difficult. Thus she makes a companion out of her great enemy. This is one of the turning points of the story, representing her capacity to forgive, a necessity if she is to survive long on the island. Rontu not only gives her much-needed companionship, but, when he overcomes the leader of the wild dogs, he effectively removes the pack as a menace to Karana.

Karana's relationship with Rontu marks the beginning of a significant transformation in her character. At one point, shortly after she befriends Rontu, she kills a deadly octopus, an event that would normally signify a rite of passage and engender a sense of pride. But Karana feels no sense of triumph, only a strange emptiness that she herself is at a loss to explain. She reports simply that "I saw two more giant devilfish along the reef that summer, but I did not try to spear them" (*Island,* 124). Her developing respect for animals is the logical evolution of the sensitivity she displayed earlier, in the third chapter of the book, when she expressed revulsion at the Aleuts' killing of an otter. At that time she confessed, "I was angry, for these animals were my friends" (*Island,* 16). Her love of the animal world is now extending to even those animals who could pose threats to her. It is an example of her maturity that she recognizes the world is not for human beings alone. But she has not completely divested herself of her past. On an expedition she discovers the burial place of one of her ancestors in a sea cave where she is forced to spend the night because of the rising tide. It is a frightening experience for her, although she realizes she should have nothing to fear from the bones deposited there. The entire episode is haunting with its descriptions of eerie figures with blank faces and glittering abalone discs as eyes, with a human skeleton propped "against the wall with its knees drawn up and in its fingers, which were raised to its mouth, a flute of pelican bone" (*Island,* 128). During the long night, Karana refuses to look back at the skeleton and the glittering eyes, and when she is finally able to leave, Karana dubs the place Black Cave and vows never to return. She goes home, leaving behind her the last vestigial ties to her former life. Now she readies herself for the anticipated coming of the Aleuts.

The arrival of the Aleuts poses a significant threat, but it also offers an unusual opportunity. They are accompanied by a girl named Tutok, who discovers Karana in hiding making her skirt of cormorant feathers. Karana distrusts her at first, but when Tutok gives her a gift of a necklace, she knows her secret is safe. A close bond is knit between them, and Karana even divulges to Tutok her secret name. The fact that Rontu approaches Tutok and lets her touch him tells Karana that Rontu had, indeed, been her dog, left on the island after that fateful visit so many years before. This interlude helps to maintain Karana's link with the human world, but it perhaps only deepens her loneliness when the Aleuts leave.

As time passes, Karana tames two birds and gives them names, and eventually finds a friend in an injured sea otter (originally named Mona-a-nee—"Little Boy with Large Eyes"—but changed to Won-a-nee—"Little Girl with Large Eyes"—when she shows up with baby otters). Later she adds an injured seagull to her menagerie, and, in time, she discovers that her developing relationships with animals will make it virtually impossible for her to kill any animals (save for some selected shellfish for food). Karana realizes how strange her attitude would seem to her own people: "Ulape would have laughed at me, and others would have laughed, too—my father most of all. Yet this is the way I felt about the animals who had become my friends and those who were not, but in time could be" (*Island,* 156). Karana's long life of solitude on the island has deepened her perspective and her sensitivity, and she sees that "animals and birds are like people, too, though they do not talk the same or do the same things. Without them the earth would be an unhappy place" (*Island,* 156). This is the message that O'Dell initially set out to deliver in the book, and for the first time in a major children's story we find the environmentalists' credo—that all life is sacred, that we share this earth together with all living things, and that we have an obligation to preserve the earth intact for succeeding generations.

Karana's final years on the island are compressed into a few chapters, the most touching passage being that relating the death of Rontu. The noble animal's quiet death of old age is movingly described in the simple, direct language that characterizes Karana so well:

> Slowly he walked to where I was standing and fell at my feet. I put my hand on his chest. I could feel his heart beating, but it beat only twice, very slowly, loud and hollow like the waves on the beach, and then no more. . . . I buried him on the headland. I dug a hole in the crevice of the rock, digging for two days from dawn until the going down of the sun, and put him there with some sand flowers and a stick he liked to chase when I threw it, and covered him with pebbles of many colors that I gathered on the shore. (*Island,* 160)

The book closes swiftly after this, although Karana spends several more years on the island. She befriends a dog who is almost certainly one of Rontu's offspring and survives an earthquake. Finally, a ship with white men aboard arrives to take her away from the island.

O'Dell is not often a poetic writer, but in these closing lines he achieves something quite beautiful:

> The last thing I saw of it was the high headland. I thought of Rontu lying there beneath the stones of many colors, and of Won-a-nee, wherever she was, and the little red fox that would scratch in vain at my fence, and my canoe hidden in the cave, and of all the happy days.
> Dolphins rose out of the sea and swam before the ship. They swam for many leagues in the morning through the bright water, weaving their foamy patterns. The little birds were chirping in their cage and Rontu-Aru sat beside me. (*Island,* 181)

Style

In writing *Island of the Blue Dolphins,* O'Dell was presented with the challenge of how to maintain the reader's interest when, for much of the story, only a single human being occupies the stage. That he succeeds may be attributed to the well-paced plot and to the development of Karana as a character.

As has been noted, O'Dell had come to prefer the first-person narrator, and in *Island of the Blue Dolphins* we are brought into Karana's world completely through that technique. The book reads in part like a journal, although Karana would have been incapable of keeping a written record. So long as we do not probe too far into the circumstances of her narration and how she came to be telling us this story, we can enjoy the confidence into which we have been taken by a very sensitive young woman.

O'Dell handles the novel's pacing and avoids the pitfall of tediousness through a variety of techniques. Jon Stott has pointed out that O'Dell actually delays the central character's isolation until the end of chapter 8, after Ramo has been killed.[3] This allows O'Dell to establish Karana's social milieu, to define the roots of her character, and to introduce her antagonists, the Aleuts, whom she encounters later on the island. Then O'Dell alternates accounts of Karana's daily activities, including "how-to" chapters, with episodes of extraordinary events—wrestling with the devilfish, attempting the dangerous journey to the mainland, forming a friendship with Tutok. Thus, he avoids a slackening of the pace, and the reader's interest is not allowed to wane. As Stott writes,

> O'Dell invests the lonely, often monotonous life of a young girl with significance. He presents details with graphic realism, arranges a series of symbolic events, and, from within the mind of his principal character, tells of the courage and love she uses to survive an inner loneliness which is greater than the outer dreariness of her life and of the maturing process in which hatred and fear have been replaced by love and sociality. (Stott, 446)

Island of the Blue Dolphins as Robinsonnade

In R. M. Ballantyne's *The Coral Island* (1858), the story of three English boys shipwrecked on an island in the South Seas, the boys are rescued after many harrowing adventures, and it is only then, when they are leaving for England, that they discover how deeply they have been touched by their experience:

> That night, as we sat on the taffrail gazing out upon the wide sea and up into the starry firmament, a thrill of joy, strangely mixed with sadness,

passed through our hearts; for we were at length "homeward bound," and were gradually leaving far behind us the beautiful, bright green coral islands of the Pacific Ocean.[4]

It is not surprising that these lines are echoed in the closing passage of *Island of the Blue Dolphins* quoted above. Both stories bear resemblance to that grandparent of all modern survival tales, Daniel Defoe's *Robinson Crusoe* (1719).

If *Robinson Crusoe* is not the first desert island survival story, it is certainly the most influential, as suggested by the epithet *Robinsonnade,* which has long been used to designate such works. The development of the Robinsonnade as a literary form within a society suggests that that society has attained a certain level of civilization. As Ian Watt points out, "the main processes by which man secures food, clothing, and shelter are only likely to become interesting when they have become alien to his common, everyday experience. To enjoy the description of the elementary productive processes reveals a sophisticated taste."[5] Only after division of labor had eliminated the necessity for complete self-reliance, was self-reliance itself to become a strange and appealing concept. *Robinson Crusoe,* a work intended for adults, was almost immediately popular with children, its appeal undoubtedly attributable to its exotic setting, its adventure, and its absence of any governing authority. In the traditional Robinsonnade, Stuart Hannabuss notes, "Characters always stay in control of their destiny, despite the fact that being castaway is supremely the dilemma where survival is most at risk. . . . The realism which could make this experience so much more disturbing for the reader was generally kept out."[6] In these earlier works, little attempt at psychological realism is found—neither the depression nor the introspection that we might expect from long-isolated individuals. However, it is a trait of more recent survival stories—and especially of *Island of the Blue Dolphins*—that the main character is taken to the brink of desperation, to the "very edge of disaster" (Hannabuss, 78). As readers, we become engaged in the protagonist's method of coping both physically and psychologically. In O'Dell we see this in Karana's soul-searching as she is forced to befriend an archenemy, Rontu, and later Tutok; and in her thwarted, futile effort to sail alone to the mainland.

The typical children's survival story depicts young people shifting for themselves without the help or guidance of their parents or any other adults. One notable exception is Johann David Wyss's *Swiss Family Robinson* (1812–1813). In this much-emulated stepchild of *Robinson Cru-*

soe, an entire family is stranded—father, mother, and two sons. Its appeal is in the domestic unit, and it reads as a sort of combination family novel/adventure story. It also facilitates the moral education of youth, an important element in much of Victorian children's literature. But the more common trend in the Robinsonnade for young readers is for the youthful protagonist to find him- or herself stranded in a wilderness without the advantage of adult wisdom and experience. Naturally, the reason for eliminating adults in a young reader's Robinsonnade is much the same as in any child's story. For young people to be the true central figures, they must not be seen to compete with adults for authority. They must be able to experience a degree of freedom wherein they are allowed choices. To put it simply, they must be allowed to grow up. Consequently, in most *bildungsromans,* which Robinsonnades generally are, we see the youthful protagonists making it on their own. The Victorians were drawn to the Robinsonnade because it could satisfy their curiosity about distant lands (many of which they owned), and the desert island setting could serve as a classroom in which the characters (and the readers) received instruction, not in wilderness survival techniques, but in human values. Usually, for the Victorians, those values came from appropriate doses of religion. Ballantyne's *The Coral Island* is the quintessential Victorian Robinsonnade, with young boys compelled to fend for themselves on a desert island through pirate attacks and cannibal threats, hurricanes and volcanic explosions, and, of course, the requisite shark encounter. Although the three heroes of that story do not build a colonial civilization as does Crusoe, neither do they attempt to understand the new land that proves to be their salvation. They approach their experience with the same smug self-confidence as does Crusoe, assured of their superiority over the natives as well as the animal life and persuaded that they have more to offer the strange environment than it does them.

Ballantyne's work inspired numerous similar tales, most notably R. L. Stevenson's *Treasure Island* (1883) and William Golding's *Lord of the Flies* (1954). Golding's profoundly moving work even borrows the names of Ballantyne's principal characters. But a darker philosophy informs Golding's book, which ends in tragedy and the failure of the island society. After Golding, only an unabashed sentimentalist or a satirist could write an idyllic Robinsonnade in which the protagonist presumes to govern the environment, to bend circumstances to his or her will. *Lord of the Flies* may not be for children, but Golding's vision has not been lost on modern children's writers. Even if most children's

Robinsonnades of the late twentieth century have happy endings, they are not afraid to confront some of the darker issues that would logically face their protagonists—for one, the psychological torments of depression brought about by loneliness and fear.

It is O'Dell's great contribution to this subgenre that he created a protagonist who would learn the virtue of peaceful coexistence, who would come to respect the natural world and to understand the role of human beings in the complex fabric of life. O'Dell, in his passion about the needless slaughter of animals, was one of the first children's authors to give us the survival story with an environmental message. His successors recognized the inevitable direction of the survival story, as evidenced by works such as Theodore Taylor's *The Cay* (1969), Jean Craighead George's *Julie of the Wolves* (1972), and Gary Paulsen's *Dogsong* (1985). These efforts have resulted in more credible novels and, at the same time, novels with moral messages as powerful as in any work from the impassioned pens of the Victorians.

The Legacy

In *Island of the Blue Dolphins,* O'Dell hit upon a formula long popular with young readers: a youth is left to survive alone on a deserted isle (or some other suitably isolated place) with only animals for company. This scenario offers the opportunity both for excitement as the protagonist faces the physical hardships of an unyielding environment and for introspection as he or she faces the psychological challenges of isolation from other human beings. It also presents one of the great enticements of childhood, that of "a glorious freedom away from the constraints of civilized life" (Hannabuss, 71). Moreover, for O'Dell the form brings the advantage so prized by the Victorians—it gives "wide flexibility to authors, who [can] excite, educate, and admonish through its pages, and who [can] reflect current interests and values there too" (Hannabuss, 81). O'Dell's instruction is not in wilderness survival techniques, as interesting as they are, but rather in human values, for here, on the edge of civilization, we discover what really matters in life. Here we can put our own existence into the proper perspective with that of the rest of nature. O'Dell arrives at a very different set of values than did his Victorian precursors, values that glorify not the achievements of humankind but the wonders of the wide and varied world around us.

Charles Dickens wrote of *Robinson Crusoe* that it was the "only instance of a universally popular book that could make no one laugh and no one cry."[7] It is difficult to say how many readers of *Island of the Blue Dolphins* are moved to tears—but if readers do not weep, it is only because they have gained strength from Karana's stoicism, her inner strength that will not allow her to fall into sentimentalism. In contrast to Defoe's book, O'Dell's survival tale exudes a poignancy and dignity that the author was never to equal again. Austin Olney, O'Dell's long-time friend and his first editor at Houghton Mifflin, has remarked that *Island of the Blue Dolphins* seemed to fly off Scott O'Dell's pen as if guided by the muses—it was a "gift of the Gods."[8] Few would disagree with that assessment. O'Dell would write more exciting books and more complex stories but none more beautiful or more deeply moving.

Chapter Four
Stories from the Old Southwest

{T}he sound of the sea and the feel of the frontier are in my books.
—O'Dell, quoted in *Something about the Author* (1990)

The publication of *Island of the Blue Dolphins* in 1960 was just the beginning of a remarkable career for Scott O'Dell. Although several years passed before his next book was completed, award-winning books poured from his pen through the late 1960s and into the early 1970s. Most of his early children's books focus on the Old Southwest, the land and history he knew and loved best. This chapter will examine the works from this period, as well as two books from the mid-1970s—*Zia,* the long-awaited sequel to *Island of the Blue Dolphins,* and *Carlota,* his last historical novel about this region.

The King's Fifth

The King's Fifth, O'Dell's second novel for young readers, was published in 1966. It is the story of an ill-fated Spanish expedition in search of the seven cities of gold in the early sixteenth century, told by a young cartographer who miraculously survives the ordeal. Structurally, *The King's Fifth* is a more complex work than *Island of the Blue Dolphins.* O'Dell uses the device of a story within a story, with the framing story consisting of the narrator's experiences in a Spanish prison in New Spain and the story within the story describing the expedition itself. The narrator, Estéban de Sandoval, is determined to commit his experiences to paper in order that "I may find the answer to all that puzzles me. God willing, I shall find my way through the labyrinth which leads to the lair of the minotaur."[1] Thus the story becomes a means for the young narrator to achieve an understanding of his ordeal and, he hopes, a way to expiation. Readers of the novel will note, in addition to its more complex design, a more sophisticated vocabulary and style than in *Island of the Blue Dolphins,* a style that befits an educated Spaniard of the sixteenth century.

The framing story opens in a Spanish prison in sixteenth-century New Spain, where Estéban de Sandoval is awaiting trial for allegedly withholding the king's due of one-fifth of any treasure recovered from the fabled Cíbola—the seven cities of gold. Unscrupulous jailers attempt to persuade Estéban to share his treasure with them in return for aiding his escape. Meanwhile, Estéban, attempting to purge his soul, recounts in writing his own recollections of the events that brought him to the prison in the first place, and this tale becomes the embedded narrative. He writes at night, and these flashback chapters alternate with the chapters describing his equally unpleasant experiences with the Spanish legal system.

The embedded narrative proceeds as follows: Estéban comes to the New World from Seville as a cartographer, intending initially to work for Coronado, but he is enticed by the crafty Captain Mendoza to join his expedition and be the first to map the newly discovered lands that now make up the American Southwest. Mendoza is driven by lust for gold, whereas Estéban's is a lust for fame, but both appetites are manifestations of the destructive greed that plagues human beings. Despite being outnumbered, the Spaniards, with their vastly superior weapons, defeat the Indians and claim the Great Abyss (the Grand Canyon) for Spain's Charles V. They continue their explorations and eventually do find gold, which they steal from the Indians. But the sacrifice is great: all of the Spaniards eventually die, either in battle or in the desert, save for Estéban. By now Estéban has realized what a curse the gold has become, and he disposes of it. On his return to New Spain, he is arrested and charged, which brings us to the point where the framing story begins.

Mendoza is a powerful figure, one of O'Dell's contemptuous villains, in the vein of Don Saturnino (*Hill of the Hawk*) and Don Ruiz (*The Sea Is Red*), obsessed with greed and power. He is cruel, insensitive, and possessed by a singleness of purpose: to find the gold. At one point, the expedition arrives at a place called the Red House, reputed to be one of the seven cities of gold, only to find a dusty ruin, which ominously foreshadows their destiny. Mendoza's response to the native peoples at the Red House is simply to shoot them. He has equally little regard for his own men. His greed overcomes him, and he plots against his fellow soldiers to increase his share of the treasure. With appropriate irony, Mendoza is killed by a dog whom he himself had trained to attack.

Acting as a foil to the cruel, rapacious nature of Mendoza is Zia, an Indian girl who serves as guide and interpreter. Estéban first mistakes

Zia for a boy because of her appearance, but she soon sets him straight with her characteristic directness and occasionally sharp tongue. She is another of O'Dell's strong female characters, in the mold of Karana, Marta, and Carlota. Zia's independence is demonstrated by her desire to ride a horse despite the tribal customs that forbid it. She eventually gets her way. She is intrigued by Estéban's drawing and coloring of his maps, and the two become friends. The expedition will more than once be indebted to Zia for its survival, but she is sickened by the violence and avarice of the Spaniards and ultimately is compelled to leave them. Zia meets Estéban again at the story's close when she is brought before the Spanish Audiencia that is trying Estéban and is questioned about the gold. She tells the truth—the gold was found at the bottom of a lake and reputedly came down from a mountain by way of a stream. When she is asked if she could find the City of Tawhi, where this mountain is, she responds firmly, "I will never go to the City of Tawhi again. . . . With the soldiers or without them. Never again" (*Fifth*, 241). This is indicative of her moral principles and her strength of character. Upon leaving the interrogation, she can only say to Estéban, "I hope that my words did not harm you with the judge." He replies simply, "You spoke the truth" (*Fifth*, 242). Pure of heart and intelligent, Zia is the moral standard against which all the characters—Estéban included—ultimately must be measured and found wanting. It should be noted that like Zia the rest of the Indians do not value the gold as the Spaniards do, and they are perplexed by the Spaniards' obsessions. The natives, who possess the gold but are not possessed by it, bring into relief the misguided values of the Spanish conquerors.

The expedition party includes Father Francisco, whose mission is to convert the Indians they encounter and tend to the spiritual needs of the Spaniards. The priest is essentially well meaning and a pacifist. When he is told that "The matchlock speaks louder than pious words," he responds, "It speaks a language which I do not understand" (*Fifth*, 121). His attempts to convert the natives are futile, and at times he cuts a slightly ridiculous figure in his missionary zeal, completely failing to comprehend the Indians' spiritual needs. He attempts to tell them the story of the Resurrection, but the idea of a man rising from the dead makes no sense to them. He succeeds in distilling for them one of the fundamental messages of the Gospels: "[Jesus] told the people many things, but what He told them mostly was this—Love one another" (*Fifth*, 127). Of course, the irony is that the Spaniards themselves do not comprehend Father Francisco's message: They are the true lost souls.

This is but one example of O'Dell's thinly veiled attack on institutionalized Christianity, which he faults for its hypocrisy and its ineffectuality, but perhaps most for its intolerance of native ways and its role in the suppression of native tribes. The priest, on the other hand, is the one Spaniard who does not fall under the spell of the gold. After Mendoza's death, when only Estéban, Zia, and Father Francisco remain, the priest wants to bury the gold, but Estéban is now sick with gold fever and insists on taking it with them, even though its burden is exceedingly taxing. Father Francisco dies shortly thereafter, and his death weighs heavily on Estéban's conscience.

Estéban is one of O'Dell's more fully developed characters. He begins the journey as an innocent mapmaker who has more in common with Zia and Father Francisco than with Mendoza. Once, during an ambush, Estéban is given a matchlock gun, but he protests, "I'm a cartographer . . . not a soldier" (Fifth, 84). He then finds himself in hand-to-hand combat with an Indian youth, during which Estéban gains the upper hand but cannot bring himself to slay the young man. Mendoza intervenes and kills the youth himself. Estéban is shaken; he sees lying before him "a young man, scarcely older than I. We could have been friends who had paused to rest beside the road after a long journey" (Fifth, 92). But as time progresses, we see him growing more and more like Mendoza, intimidating and deceiving the Indians they encounter, undergoing tremendous hardship for the sake of the bags of gold they carry. His transformation sickens Zia, and because of it she departs.

When Father Francisco dies, Estéban at last is awakened to the change that threatens to overwhelm him. Filled with remorse and guilt over the priest's death, Estéban laments that the gold "is the cause of your death and the guilt for your death is mine" (Fifth, 254). To rid himself of the burden—both physical and spiritual—he dumps the gold into a sulfurous spring, an act that will only partly expiate his sin. He heads toward Culiacán, carrying with him the book of pressed flowers that Father Francisco had gathered during his sojourn. The priest's gathering of flowers symbolizes his gentle nature, but it also may suggest his desire to learn something of the new land rather than merely to ravage it as Mendoza had done. In that respect, he shares an interest with Estéban and his wish to map the country, although in Father Francisco we see none of the quest for fame that for a time grips the young Estéban. In Culiacán Estéban finds himself under arrest for evading the king's tax.

Estéban is a very human figure who succumbs, if briefly, to temptation. He lacks the strength of Zia and the faith of Father Francisco, but he can learn from both. It is in the framing story that we see Estéban's maturation. While in prison, he learns that he is being tried not only for withholding the king's fifth, but also for the murder of Mendoza, a crime that carries a certain death sentence. Zia appears as a surprise witness to exonerate him, but she cannot forgive his avaricious behavior. And so, absolved of the murder, Estéban is sentenced to only three years for withholding the king's fifth. He rejects an offer by the prison captain to let him escape in return for sharing the gold. This action is the final sign of his emergence into maturity; he is now a strong and secure figure with the intelligence to recognize evil and the courage to resist it. Estéban now realizes that true freedom exists only if his soul is free from the bondage of greed and lust for glory. He gladly decides to serve out his three-year sentence for that absolution.

In many respects, *The King's Fifth* is like a parable denouncing the evil of gold. (O'Dell's next work, *The Black Pearl,* is best described as a parable on the same general theme—the danger of lust and greed.) John Rowe Townsend notes that the very idea of treasure is "sinister": "It is not merely that treasure is often both hidden and discovered in circumstances of violence and treachery. The truth is also that the hope of great unearned gain can be one of the most corrupting ever to get men in its grip. In *The King's Fifth* there are not so much good and bad characters as the innocent and the corrupted."[2] For the most part, the Indians are portrayed as innocent and the Spaniards as corrupted. One critic points to this as a flaw, lending the book a lack of balance that denies "the realities of human nature" (Usrey, 282). A similar lack of balance affects some of O'Dell's later work—*Sing Down the Moon, Zia,* and the Seven Serpents Trilogy, particularly. But one suspects O'Dell would not have apologized for this transgression; for him it was an overdue tribute to Native Americans so long the victims in their own land. It is important to note that the Spanish corruption goes beyond mere avarice. The society seems corrupted through and through. The legal system, where we would expect to find justice, is hopelessly diseased. During Estéban's stay in the dreaded fortress of San Juan de Ulúa in Vera Cruz, his cell is frequented by government officials of all ranks, each attempting to persuade Estéban to share the secret of the gold in return for his release. Those who administer the king's justice are little interested in truth and less interested in justice. Judgments can be purchased, freedom can be bargained for, and no one can be trusted.

The King's Fifth, one of O'Dell's longest and most complex books for young readers, requires patience. The initial chapters unfold slowly, and the book is populated with thoroughly disagreeable characters, making its mood somber, at times almost oppressive. But the exploration of moral choices is penetrating—the best O'Dell will ever do. The character of Estéban is one of his finest creations, fully realized and happily believable. And the suspense increases in both the embedded story and in the framing story as the novel progresses. The book deserves the accolades it received from early reviewers: "Unloose the adjectives for [*The King's Fifth*]: a stunning novel of compelling interest and mounting impact."³ John Rowe Townsend's assessment was the most enthusiastic when he wrote in 1971 that "*The King's Fifth*—a sombre, almost stately novel—is his best of all" (Townsend, 282). If subsequent history has not sustained that judgment—at least in most eyes—few readers would deny the book's power and insight. It is O'Dell still at the height of his craft.

The Black Pearl

The Black Pearl appeared in 1967, just one year after *The King's Fifth*. It bears many similarities to that work in its theme, setting, and characterization, but the approach and style are dramatically different. Whereas *The King's Fifth* is clearly historical fiction, *The Black Pearl* can best be described as a fable, with a timeless setting and archetypal figures. It is the story of Ramón, the son of Blas Salazar, a pearl merchant from Baja California, who discovers the legendary black pearl, known to local inhabitants as the Pearl of Heaven, which he takes from the cave of a great manta, the Manta Diablo. El Diablo is itself a legendary creature, whose name strikes terror in children—a fact that mothers use to their advantage on their more unruly offspring. The pearl is the most magnificent Blas Salazar has ever seen, and with his deft touch Salazar peels away the pearl's outer layer and removes its only flaw. What remains is a huge, perfect work. But when dealers try to cheat him out of a fair price for the pearl, Salazar gives it to the statue of the Madonna in the local church. Salazar's great sin is that he gave the gift out of anger and not out of love. He hopes, as well, that his gift to the Virgin will buy him favor from heaven. But shortly afterward, he and his entire fleet of ships are destroyed in a fierce storm. The sole survivor of the catastrophe is a mysterious diver, Gaspar Ruiz, known as the Sevillano, who is determined to have the pearl for himself. Ramón, now persuaded of the pearl's curse, retrieves it from the church before the Sevillano can steal it and is determined to return it to El Diablo. A deadly pursuit follows, taking them to the mouth of the great sea cave wherein El Diablo lives. In a dramatic confrontation that is reminiscent of Captain Ahab struggling with the great white whale, the Sevillano is taken to his doom on the back of the Manta Diablo, leaving Ramón with the pearl, which he returns to the Madonna. Unlike his father's gift, Ramón's is one of love and therefore blessed.

The story's stark simplicity, the clear demarcation between good and evil, and the emphasis on reward and punishment all contribute to its fable-like qualities. The characters are few and sharply delineated. Ramón Salazar, the narrator, is an innocent, unassuming youth poised to enter manhood. Blas Salazar is a successful, if somewhat arrogant, businessman—although his arrogance is perhaps encouraged by his success. Gaspar Ruiz, who calls himself the Sevillano because he claims to come from Seville, is a proud and greedy diver of unsavory reputation in the Salazars' employ. Soto Luzon is an old Indian diver who has long sold pearls to the Salazars; it is to him that Ramón turns when he wishes to learn how to dive, and the superstitious Luzon is also most familiar with the Manta Diablo. Not the least of the characters is the Manta Diablo itself, whose presence looms over the story like that of Moby-Dick. El Diablo—the devil—becomes a symbolic and ominous creature exerting an awesome power over the principal characters. The allusions to *Moby-Dick* are probably not accidental, since Melville's masterpiece was a favorite of O'Dell's and would form the basis for his next book, *The Dark Canoe*.

Not surprisingly, the tale is rife with symbols. The characters themselves are archetypal. The Sevillano represents the cardinal sins of pride and avarice. He only spares Ramón after he snatches the pearl from him because he believes that the Salazar name will garner a higher price for the gem. The Sevillano's appearance would seem to belie his inner character:

> He was tall and his shoulders were so wide and powerful that they seemed to be armored in steel instead of muscle. His hair, which was gold-colored, grew thick on his head like a helmet. He had blue eyes, so blue and handsome that any girl would have envied them. His face was handsome, too, except that around his mouth there always lurked the shadow of a sneer.[4]

The one other notable physical feature is his tattoos, scenes of his heroic exploits—his fight with an octopus, his stabbing a charging bull, his choking a mountain lion—"he looked very much like a picture gallery walking around" (*Pearl*, 19). These tattoos are visible expressions of his pridefulness, and we are naturally wont to believe the exploits they advertise are pure fabrications. They do foreshadow his death in the embrace of the great Manta Diablo. In his dying, he becomes, in fact, the hero he always believed himself to be. His boasting becomes reality. The Sevillano, if cast slightly differently, could be a classical tragic hero—strong, handsome, powerful, determined, and, at last, done in by his own unyielding pride. But his particularly villainous quality is his mendacity. Everything about the Sevillano is deception, from the tattoos that do not depict real accomplishments to his moniker, for he had never set foot in Seville.

From the beginning, Blas Salazar recognizes the Sevillano as a troublemaker, but at the same time he acknowledges his great skill—"he is the best gatherer of pearls we have" (*Pearl*, 23)—and because of that Salazar is willing to wink at his shortcomings. Salazar is a much-admired businessman. He drives a hard bargain, is fair in his business dealings, and, like any shrewd entrepreneur, is willing to take risks in hopes of reaping financial rewards. He is also skilled in all facets of his profession. His deft touch removes the flawed outer layers of nacre from the giant pearl, making it a perfect specimen. Peeling is a technique commonly used to remove blemishes from pearls, and O'Dell may simply have wanted to describe the process. However, by peeling the pearl, Salazar attempts to improve upon nature. And, when he meets his own destruction in a great storm, it is in part because he allowed greed to cloud his judgment, which resulted in an arrogant attitude toward nature. In the end, nature will always win—at least in an O'Dell book.

Soto Luzon is a foil to the Sevillano: He is scrupulously honest in his dealings with the Salazars, and, more important, he harbors a great respect for El Diablo and the other mysteries of nature. Whereas the Sevillano (and Salazar to some extent) believes that he can exert power over the forces of nature, and, in fact, over the Deity, Luzon knows better. Ramón calls him superstitious, but that is another way of saying that he is humble before the greater powers in the universe. Luzon knows El Diablo well—his haunts, his habits, his comings and goings. He also keeps a pact with El Diablo, whom Luzon believes to have supernatural attributes, including the ability to transform himself into human form and walk the streets. Luzon possesses the same attitude toward the natural world that Karana adopted after many lonely years on the island.

Soto Luzon acts as spiritual adviser to Ramón, a role that, interestingly enough, cannot be filled by the village priest, Father Gallardo. Father Gallardo, in fact, is the antithesis of the almost ethereal Luzon. The priest is the embodiment of the worldliness of the Roman Catholic Church—his blessing on the Salazars is to "[s]peed them to the pearling grounds and bring them safely home. We ask that You bless the House of Salazar that has so honored our church this day, that they may find another pearl as large as the one they have given" (*Pearl,* 58). Luzon, on the other hand, has a special affinity with nature and is in tune to its rhythms. Only Luzon does not fear the Manta Diablo: "I show him proper respect and tip my hat when I come into the lagoon and when I leave it. For this he allows me to dive for the black pearls which belong to him . . ." (*Pearl,* 34). Ramón must reconcile the teachings of Luzon, whom he greatly respects, with those of the church in whose traditions he has been raised. Readers of O'Dell will recognize his antipathy to institutionalized religion. This is the most pointed criticism of the church O'Dell had yet leveled in one of his children's stories, but it would not be the last, nor the most severe. Nonetheless, O'Dell's theme of the true nature of giving is a religious one, and *The Black Pearl* glows with a religious aura.

In the final chapter, Ramón returns home alone after the dramatic struggle with the giant manta and with the Sevillano. The first place he goes upon reaching town is the church, where he restores the pearl to the Madonna-of-the-Sea and says, "This now is a gift of adoration . . . a gift of love" (*Pearl,* 95). Then he says "a prayer for the soul of the Sevillano and one for my own. I also said a prayer for the Manta Diablo, that creature of beauty and of evil whom only two have seen with their eyes, though there are many who say they have and whom everyone in this life at sometimes comes to know" (*Pearl,* 95). These are the words of a mature 16-year-old, and we see this story as a *bildungsroman*—as are so many of O'Dell's novels. Ramón has learned the lesson of humility in the face of nature's beautiful, but sometimes destructive, forces. He has learned the lesson of the power of love and the importance of forgiveness. Without forgiveness, there can be no love. Thus Ramón's gift of the pearl to the Virgin must be sanctified by his prayers for the souls of his enemies. He rings the big bells of the church to summon the villagers so they will know the pearl has been restored. But Ramón slips away unnoticed. He has no need of public accolades: "Outside, the sun now lay golden on the roof tops and the big bells were still ringing over the town. They rang in my heart, also, for this new day was the beginning day of my manhood. It was not the day I became a partner in the House of Salazar nor the day I found the Pearl of Heaven. It was this day" (*Pearl,* 95 –96). *The Black Pearl* contains some of O'Dell's finest passages. Ramón's struggle with the Sevillano and El Diablo is one of his most exciting scenes. The striking imagery of the Pearl of Heaven, the terrible Manta Diablo, and the implacable sea combine to create a wonderfully charged tale pitting good against evil, love against selfishness, humility against pride. These themes are always close to O'Dell's heart, and he would continue to explore them in his succeeding works. For this book O'Dell received a richly deserved second Newbery Honor citation.

Sing Down the Moon

In 1970, O'Dell's third Newbery Honor book appeared. In *Sing Down the Moon,* O'Dell returns to historical fiction with a story based on the Long Walk, the forced migration in 1864 of the Navahos from their Arizona homeland to Fort Sumner, New Mexico, at the hands of the American government. Once again, as in *Island of the Blue Dolphins,* O'Dell portrays a strong woman as his central character, the narrator Bright Morning. At the story's opening, Bright Morning, a Navaho girl of about 15, is tending her family's sheep and chatting gaily with her friends, White Deer and Running Bird. All three admire a lithe and handsome young brave, Tall Boy, who is regarded as a potential husband for Bright Morning. After all, he is the most eligible bachelor in the village, and her mother has the largest sheep herd. (In the Navaho nation, the women own the sheep, which are the most valuable possessions.) Tall Boy has been proving his prowess by leading a raid on the neighboring Utes, against the express orders of the American soldiers. This prepares us for the tragedy of the forced migration later in the book.

However, the mesa offers more than one kind of danger, for Bright Morning and Running Bird are kidnapped by Spanish slavers and taken to a town in Mexico where they become house servants. Most of the first half of the book consists of the story of their Mexican captivity. O'Dell seems to be emphasizing that the race of one's captors is irrelevant, that people of all nations, ethnic backgrounds, and creeds can perpetrate violence. When Bright Morning and Running Bird first reach the town, they are greeted with the frantic cry of a young Nez Percé girl, "Run, run, even though they kill you. It is better to die on the street."[5] Death, in other words, is preferable to slavery. The girl, who has also been captured by the Mexicans, is called Nehana, and she and Bright Morning form a bond and draw strength from each other. The three girls hatch a plot to escape during the hubbub of the Easter festivities—which are interestingly related through the eyes of Bright Morning, a cultural outsider. They are pursued on their flight by some Spaniards, but are rescued by Tall Boy, who is severely wounded in the process.

Their arrival home provides a brief, peaceful interlude before the second half of the story begins, that focusing on the forced migration. Tall Boy's wound has resulted in his losing use of his arm—a crushing blow for a promising warrior and hunter, who must now be confined to sitting with women, weaving, cutting wood, and shearing sheep. It is particularly disappointing to Bright Morning's family, but Bright Morning herself has only grown closer to Tall Boy. Her capacity to overlook Tall Boy's physical debilities suggests her growth as a person. This growth is further emphasized in the chapter describing Bright Morning's Womanhood Ceremony, a four-day rite of passage during which many demands are made of her, all designed to instill industry, obedience, and comeliness. It climaxes with a race, which she is contrived to win. By describing this Navaho tradition, O'Dell helps the reader gain an understanding of the culture, thereby developing sympathy for the Navahos in their plight at the hands of the American soldiers.

Shortly after the ceremony, the American soldiers, or Long Knives as the Navahos call them, inform the villagers that they must leave their land. The Navahos resist, escaping to the mesa where they hold out as long as they can. Their village is burned, and they are at last taken captive and begin a march that is beset by grim hardships. Death is all around them, food is scarce, the rigors of the march exhausting. Bright Morning watches her grandmother die, and a little girl who is placed in her charge by a desperate mother dies in her arms. When they reach their destination at Bosque Redondo, they are fed wheat, which upsets their digestive systems, so they are ill much of the time. In addition, they are idle, which makes them miserable, and they live in constant fear of being massacred by the whites.

Amid this hardship, Bright Morning marries Tall Boy and becomes pregnant. She vows to return to their canyon, but Tall Boy, who has lost much of his verve, is reluctant. Only through Bright Morning's persistence is Tall Boy at last persuaded to risk fleeing. On the trail back they encounter more hardships, as well as the birth of their son, but they finally settle in a hidden canyon and recover some of the sheep that were once theirs. The conclusion has much of the flavor of romance, but their future appears bleak—a family of three, isolated from their people and living in a rugged and often unfriendly country. Of course, in time the Navahos would be permitted to return to their home in the Canyon de Chelly (in what is now Four Corners country), but they would never effectively recover from the desolating losses they suffered during the relocation. *Sing Down the Moon* is one of O'Dell's saddest stories and one of his most blatant attacks on the arrogance and insensitivity of the European Americans in their oppression of the Native Americans. We have the sense in reading this work that O'Dell is consciously trying to right a grievous wrong. We are made to feel the pain and suffering of the Navahos because the callous soldiers did not.

Two predominant themes are found in *Sing Down the Moon:* the pervasiveness of human injustice and the resilience of the individual in the face of this injustice. The injustice is a direct result of human greed for power and money, represented by the Mexicans and Americans, both of whom resort to inhumane acts to achieve their ends. The lot of the weak and powerless, in this case the Navahos, is oppression, suffering, and death. O'Dell can offer little hope in this tale—he cannot, after all, alter history. But he clearly suggests that Bright Morning's strength must derive from her heritage, the values and traditions of her people. All her hope for the future must be built upon these cultural roots. We will see this theme recur most notably in *Zia*.

The book was generally praised for its appropriately simple style, recalling Karana's narrative in *Island of the Blue Dolphins*. Indeed, Bright Morning is a figure that bears favorable comparison to Karana in the strength of her spirit and in her determination in the face of tremendous suffering. And, like Karana, Bright Morning tells her harrowing story, in the words of one reviewer, "almost devoid of emotion."[6] This, for example, is Bright Morning's account of the death of the baby in her arms:

> The night was half over and I was sitting beside the fire with the little girl in my arms. She held one of my fingers tight in her small fist and I was singing a song to her about a bird in a pine tree. I sang another song to her and another before I was aware that she was no longer listening, that she had died quietly in my arms. (*Sing,* 100)

The very absence of passion speaks of the numbness that long suffering brings, for this is one of hundreds of deaths that the Navahos experienced during this period. And the simple, direct language seems perfectly suited to a young woman whose principal desires in life are to herd her sheep, raise her son, and care for her husband in peace. In her review, Zena Sutherland wrote that the "very simplicity of [O'Dell's] writing, at times almost terse, makes more vivid the tragedy of the eviction and the danger and triumph of the return."[7] The book closes with a family portrait in which Bright Morning, tending sheep with her son, catches a glimpse of Tall Boy waving at them from the cave that is their home: "I waved back at him and hurried across the meadow. I raised my face to the falling rain. It was Navaho rain" (*Sing,* 134). This is a scene of quiet rejoicing. They are free and living on their and their ancestors' land—a modest triumph, perhaps, but that, O'Dell seems to be saying, is the nature of living.

Zia

Zia is ostensibly the sequel to *Island of the Blue Dolphins,* although it stands as a story on its own and did not appear until 1976, 16 years after the first book. O'Dell was prompted to write *Zia* by countless requests from fans of *Island of the Blue Dolphins* for the story of Karana after her rescue. But it was not in O'Dell to fabricate history, and the facts were that Karana survived only a short while after being brought to the mainland. Focusing on Karana would give O'Dell little to work with; so he chose to make Karana's niece, Zia, the protagonist. Karana, in fact, appears only briefly near the close of the book, and her death is almost pitiable in light of the sad, heroic life she led as recounted in *Island of the Blue Dolphins.*

Zia is the daughter of Karana's older sister, Ulape, who has died and left Zia and her brother, Mando, orphans residing at Santa Barbara Mission. From the outset, Zia is obsessed with rescuing her aunt from the Island of the Blue Dolphins. She and Mando claim an abandoned boat, rename it *Island Girl* (in honor of Karana), and plan to sail for the island themselves. They are given the reluctant blessing of Captain Nidever, a sailor who has once been to the island, but was unsuccessful in locating Karana. He promises to go again when he gets a business deal settled, but Zia and Mando cannot wait. Their journey is a failure, but filled with excitement. First they wrestle with a marlin for more than a day before Zia takes pity on the creature and cuts the line, to her brother's dismay. In this act we see echoes of Karana's love of wildlife, although Zia's motivation is not so readily understood. Shortly, they encounter a whaler, the *Boston Bay,* and the sailors recognize Zia's boat as one that they have lost. Zia and Mando are captured and put to work. They escape from the *Boston Bay* under cover of darkness (however, Mando, who reminds of us Karana's fearless brother, Ramo, rather relishes the idea of a whaling adventure). When they finally reach the mainland in their boat, they meet Captain Nidever, who is about to set sail for the Island of the Blue Dolphins to bring their aunt back to them. The book is nearly half over, and many readers will have the feeling that the first 10 chapters have gotten nowhere—Zia is back on the California coast still longing to rescue her aunt, and there is no sign of Karana.

Captain Nidever refuses Zia's plea to accompany him, but he does agree to take Father Vicente, a kindly priest from the mission. After Nidever leaves for the island, Zia suddenly has a thought: "What if the men found Karana on the island and brought her back with them to the Mission and she did not like the Mission, nor her new life, nor us? She would be used to her own ways on the island, doing what she wanted and living as she wanted to live. . . . It was a strange thought. It made me unhappy and kept me from going to sleep."[8] Zia's hauntings foreshadow Karana's feelings and, it turns out, her own—for this is Zia's story and not Karana's.

Halfway through the book, we are introduced to a secondary plot, the struggle between the Indians who live at the mission and the whites, including the clerics of the mission and soldiers of the garrison. The leader of the Indians (we are never told the name of their nation or tribe) is a young rebel named Gito Cruz, but called by all who know him Stone Hands. Stone Hands, who unsuccessfully courts Zia, has devised a plan to liberate the Indians at the mission. Zia's obsession with her aunt and her generally conservative nature prevent her from fleeing from the mission, but she does agree to help the others escape by unlocking the dormitory doors at night.

Her complicity in the Indians' escape and her refusal to divulge their whereabouts result in her incarceration for several days. She has no allies, neither in Captain Cordova, commander of the Mexican garrison, nor in Father Merced, the stern, uncompassionate head of the mission. Only when Captain Nidever and Father Vicente return with her aunt is Zia released. The runaways have been cornered in a box canyon and the whites hope to use Zia to entreat them to return to the mission.

Karana's return is likely to be disappointing to fans of *Island of the Blue Dolphins*. Because Zia tells the story, and because no one speaks Karana's language, we discover very little of what Karana is thinking or feeling. At first she is enthralled by the wild horses and such simple things as the taste of melon and learning to weave, but soon Karana's inability to communicate with anyone creates a profound emptiness. It is one thing to be alone on a desert island with only the animals for companionship, but quite another to be lonely in the company of other human beings and surrounded by an alien culture. Sleeping in a bed is unsettling for her, and so she lies out in the open with her dog, Rontu-Aru. Her instincts are true as ever as she leads the runaway band of Indians away from a deadly wildfire in her final heroic act. Karana herself leaves the mission for a nearby sea cave where she cares for stricken animals and finally falls ill herself. She dies, Zia believes, from homesickness and is buried at the mission. Mando has left the mission to follow Stone Hands, and Zia is now alone. Her aunt left her two things—the necklace of black stones and Rontu-Aru. Zia, who now realizes that her place is not at this mission but with her own people in her own land, leaves for the long trek home accompanied by Rontu-Aru. Just as Karana, taken from her homeland, was unable to survive in a strange land, Zia comes to understand that she can never be happy at the mission. She must return to her people to rediscover herself.

As in *Sing Down the Moon,* O'Dell emphasizes the importance of one's cultural heritage as a means of achieving identity and self-actualization. Karana, in fact, dies when she is brought to the mainland and finds herself bereft of her cultural roots. Zia, learning from her aunt's tragic experience, realizes that her greatest strength will come from a reacquaintance with her heritage and the traditions of her people. It is in the stories about Native Americans that O'Dell chiefly employs the theme of returning to one's roots for spiritual rediscovery; he certainly recognized and felt deeply the scars of genocide.

The story of *Zia* dramatizes the callous and insensitive treatment of the Indians at the hands of the missionaries and the Mexican soldiers. Driven off their land by the invaders, the Indians are forced to turn to the missions, which are ill equipped to handle them. There they are treated virtually as slaves, even being locked in their dormitories by night. O'Dell provides us the portrait of one compassionate priest, Father Vicente, but the others, Father Merced and his successor, Father Malatesta, are rigid and narrow-minded, with little understanding of the Indians or their culture. O'Dell seldom casts the church in an entirely favorable light, perhaps because he knew too well its role in the oppression of southwestern Native Americans. However, O'Dell does not create a world of clearly defined choices and easily recognizable distinctions. He portrays both the Native Americans and the Spanish missionaries as completely human, neither totally right nor wrong. As one critic puts it, "[The novel's] main skill and originality lies in using, as American teenage novels often do, the haphazardness of life, apparently random moments picked from a rich choice, a mixture of cultures, oddities of life-style."[9]

Reviewers and critics have wisely chosen not to treat *Zia* as a sequel to *Island of the Blue Dolphins*. In the lingo of television, *Zia* is a spin-off rather than a true sequel. Its principal weakness is a lack of focus. The search for Karana—which seems to be the initial plot thrust—is interrupted by an adventure on a whaling vessel and a Native American uprising against the Spanish missionaries. When Karana is finally brought to the mission, it is without the help of Zia—her earlier efforts having been for naught. The book's principal strength derives from the character of Zia, who possesses determination and deep conviction. As her character develops, she achieves a sense of identity and purpose in life. *Zia* pales beside *Island of the Blue Dolphins,* but it can be justly admired for its revelations about human nature and the need for rediscovering our roots, finding our inner strength, sharing our grief, and acting out our passion.

Carlota

In *The Year of Decision: 1846,* Bernard DeVoto's history of political and military events of the United States at the beginning of the Mexican War, the author has this to report of a skirmish in southern California:

> The action of December 6, known as the battle of San Pascual [sic], lasted only a few minutes. The revolutionaries were California horsemen, the best in the world, riding their own well-trained, fresh horses and armed with muskets and long lances. The American force was mounted on the surviving, dilapidated mules and horses, not only starving but less than half-broken, and a quarter of it was on foot. The night of rain had made firearms all but useless. A small advance guard surprised the Californians but was ridden to pieces and its commander, Captain Johnston, was killed. The main body, led by [Brigadier General Stephen Watts] Kearny, drove the Californians away and began a pursuit. The half-dead horses strung out in a long line and the Californians turned and came back. For something like five minutes there was a vicious melee of cavalry sabers and clubbed muskets against lances. When the howitzers, dragged all this way from Santa Fe for just such a use, came up the Californians rode away. They got one howitzer, however, for its team stampeded.

The little fight was as desperate as it was brief. At the end of it eigh-
teen Americans were dead [including several officers, and Kearny himself
was wounded].[10]

Upon this brief episode Scott O'Dell builds the story of *Carlota* (1977), a
tale of a strong-willed and capable young woman in the California frontier at the time of the Mexican War. O'Dell had written about the Mexican War at least twice before. In his nonfictional reminiscence *The
Cruise of the Arctic Star* (1973), he describes the Battle of San Pasqual,
focusing particularly on the exploits of the legendary Kit Carson. And
many years before, in his second novel for adults, *Hill of the Hawk,*
O'Dell had introduced a family named Zubaran, with a proud and capable daughter, Luz, an erratic father, Don Saturnino, and a colorful and
willful grandmother, Carlota. All three of these characters are resurrected in slightly different guises in *Carlota* (he even retains the family
name, but adds an acute accent to the last syllable—Zubarán—and he
gives his youthful heroine the name Carlota, renaming the grandmother
Dona Dolores). We are not to suppose, however, that the characters are
intended to be the same. They are not. But the two books do share some
similar themes, and occasionally a scene from *Carlota* will recall one
from *Hill of the Hawk.*

Carlota's story is modeled loosely on that of the historical figure Luisa
de Montero. Carlota Zubarán, the protagonist and the narrator, is the
daughter of a great family of California, and, in 1846, when the novel
opens, she is preparing for the wedding of her younger sister, Yris, to
Don Roberto, heir of a second great family, the Peraltas. Although, as
the elder daughter, Carlota herself might be expected to be the betrothed,
neither Carlota nor her father, Don Saturnino, whose favorite she is, will
agree to her marrying the unpleasant Don Roberto. Don Saturnino, who
has always seen Carlota as the replacement for the son he lost in an
Indian raid, is proud and intransigent. The third major character is Carlota's grandmother, Dona Dolores, an opinionated, domineering, old-
fashioned woman, who is horrified when her granddaughter rides her
horse astride instead of sidesaddle. Dona Dolores is almost a caricature
of haughty self-importance, and she is demanding and insensitive.
When the book opens, we find her sitting in a chair and resting her feet
on the back of one of her servants, Rosario, as if he were a footstool (a
scene drawn directly from *Hill of the Hawk,* where Dona Carlota uses her
servant, also named Rosario, for a footstool).

Very early in the book, Carlota and her father ride to nearby Blue
Beach, a secluded lagoon presumably known only to them, where a
Spanish treasure ship sank two centuries before. In the wreckage are
treasure chests filled with gold coins that supply the Zuburán family
with money in tough times. It is unclear why O'Dell felt the need to
include this incredulous detail. The treasure finances Yris's extravagant
wedding and provides Carlota an opportunity to prove her strength and
fearlessness, for it is she who does the diving. During her dive, Carlota
encounters a deadly burro clam. Similar scenes will be described in
O'Dell's later novel *Alexandra,* a modern-day tale of a diving family.

At Yris's wedding, Carlota wears pants and competes along with the
men in a race in which she narrowly defeats her new brother-in-law.
Immediately after the wedding, they hear rumors of Mojaves or Piutes
heading their way, and they expect trouble. Trouble does come, but it is
in the form of arrogant gringos. The Americans are riding stolen horses,
and Carlota manages to humiliate them by lassoing one of the horses.
However, troubles are only beginning, for shortly afterward, the American scout Kit Carson arrives at the ranch and informs them that an
American army is approaching—one that has not yet learned that the
Mexican War is over. Don Saturnino feels he has little choice but to prepare for a fight even though he is badly outnumbered. Don Saturnino
leads a band of ranchers to the attack in the valley of San Pasqual. Having no gunpowder, they carry lances. Carlota accompanies her father
despite her strong misgivings about the venture's foolhardiness. Here
Carlota is shown to be wiser than her father, but not yet strong enough
to stand up to him. She is asked to remain with the horses and so does
not fight. The battle is particularly bloody, and Carlota, from her van-
tage point, sees Kit Carson among the American soldiers. (His presence
at this skirmish is a historical fact.) In a remarkable twist of fate, the
ranchers, armed with lances and a fierce pride, defeat the American
army led by General Kearney. But Don Saturnino is severely wounded
in the contest.

After the battle, Carlota discovers an American soldier, John F. Fleming, stealing one of the horses and attempts to kill him with a lance,
succeeding only in wounding him. She takes both her father and Fleming back to the ranch. During his convalescence, Fleming tells her that
the soldiers came to bring order, not to fight. This revelation serves to
emphasize the futility of the battle and the foolish obstinacy of Don Saturnino. Don Saturnino, who had been improving, takes a sudden turn
for the worse when he learns that an American soldier is being cared for
under his own roof. Carlota, for the first time, stands up to her father,

and refuses to send the invalid Fleming away as he has demanded. Her defiance mortifies her father—literally—and he dies shortly after. Although the plot requires Don Saturnino's death, for Carlota will never fully come into her own in his lifetime, the manner of his death is likely to strike most readers as melodramatic. Don Saturnino's funeral is described almost dispassionately by Carlota; it is almost as if O'Dell had lost interest in Don Saturnino as a character.

Now in charge of the 47,000-acre ranch, Carlota faces a disastrous drought and must charge goods at Caleb Thomas's store in San Diego. Thomas attempts to take advantage of the circumstances and tries to buy Carlota's land at a rock-bottom price, and, when Dona Dolores and Carlota refuse to sell, he tries to confiscate it in payment for their debts. Carlota has no recourse but to return to Blue Beach and dive for more gold. (Clearly used as a deus ex machina, the treasure's existence may remove for some readers any sense of compassion for the characters' plight.) The story draws to a close with the beginning of the California Gold Rush, and Carlota exhibits a willingness to work with the Americans (of whom she is likely to see a great deal). She finally stands up to her overbearing grandmother and frees Rosario, the slave who had been humiliated in the old woman's service. Thus Carlota not only adapts to change, but she introduces change. This adaptability will be the key to her survival, for the Americans are taking over California, despite the Pyrrhic victory of the local ranchers at San Pasqual. The future of Carlota and her ranch depends on her ability to adjust to the dramatic transformations in store for Californian society.

Carlota has been commended for the laconic dignity of its style.[11] Its characterization, on the other hand, has been both praised and reviled. One critic, Ruth M. Stein, writes that "O'Dell creates memorable incidents rather than characters,"[12] whereas another, Malcolm Usrey, remarks that "Plot is secondary to characterization in *Carlota*" (Usrey, 289). The truth lies somewhere in between. The three main characters are sharply delineated, but predictable. We might well ask why, with such strong personalities, there are so few confrontations between them—perhaps it would have been a more interesting book if there had been. The story contains skillfully detailed and memorable scenes, that is true. Carlota's diving experience, her antics at her sister's wedding, and the exciting battle scene are all capably drawn. What is missing is a sense of cohesion. The most exciting scene, the battle, occurs two-thirds of the way through the book, which trails on for 40 more pages filled with largely forgettable incidents. Many readers will feel that the ending is overdue and wonder that it took so long for Carlota to tell off her obnoxious grandmother and to free poor Rosario from his bondage. O'Dell's portrayal of the grandmother is far more effective in *Hill of the Hawk*. Dona Carlota, in that book, possesses an irrepressible spirit and is a determined advocate for her granddaughter. Dona Dolores, on the other hand, is far less likable and comes across as simply mean-spirited.

What will stay with most readers is O'Dell's sense of place, his attachment to the California countryside, his love of and respect for the Spanish roots of the region, his belief in a strong moral fiber. Carlota's great strength derives not from the masculine traits of physical prowess and assertiveness instilled by her father, but from her own recognition of the essential worth of human beings, the sanctity of all life, and the need to act on moral principles. At the very beginning of the story, we are introduced to an eagle belonging to Don Saturnino. The proud bird is chained to a perch in the courtyard. The last act Carlota performs and the very end of the book is to file the chain and free the bird, significantly, with Rosario's assistance. (The idea of the pet eagle is also borrowed from *Hill of the Hawk,* but in that story the eagle, in a chilling piece of dramatic irony, claws its master to death.) O'Dell's abiding love of all animals pervades the novel—the horses in their beautiful strength, the fearsome and wonderful force of the burro clam, the stately eagle yearning to be free. In this final act, Carlota, like Karana, comes to understand the marvelous interplay of life in its various forms.

Conclusion

After *Island of the Blue Dolphins,* O'Dell's stories of the Old Southwest are probably his finest. He possessed an obvious affinity with the landscape and the people that is evident in none of his other works. O'Dell was not a passionate writer. Indeed, at times, he is almost maddeningly dispassionate in his drive to satisfy his story line. But when he writes of Native America—its lands and its peoples—a passion emerges. What he admires about the Native American cultures is their abiding love and respect for the natural world, their recognition of their own role in the great cycle of life. When his subject is removed from these themes, it is as if his interest flags, the spark flickers. But O'Dell also knew that never moving away from familiar themes and settings can be stultifying. So after *Sing Down the Moon* he moved into uncharted waters—for him at least. His exploration would result in some very fine stories, but he would never again quite achieve the heights that he knew with his first books for children.

Chapter Five

Experiments in Form and Substance

{T}he deepest waters are not out in the Gulf but somewhere inside you.
—O'Dell, *Alexandra* (1984)

Following his tremendous success with the southwestern historical novels of the 1960s, O'Dell perhaps worried that he was falling into a pattern and that his writing needed the stimulation of change. Beginning in the late 1960s, he engaged in a variety of literary experiments: novellas for younger audiences, a narrative travelogue, new settings for his fiction. The five works that form the focus of this chapter represent an O'Dell seeking new vehicles. From the heavy literary allusion of *The Dark Canoe* to the potpourri of *The Journey of the Arctic Star* to the tale of sixteenth-century intrigue in *The Hawk That Dare Not Hunt by Day,* these books attest to the eclecticism of O'Dell's interests and to his fertile imagination.

The Dark Canoe

Scott O'Dell loved *Moby-Dick;* it appealed to his insatiable love of the sea, his keen spirit of adventure, and his insistence on the moral obligation of literature. With his writer's confidence at a peak following the phenomenal successes since *Island of the Blue Dolphins,* O'Dell embarked on one of his most daring literary experiments, the writing of *The Dark Canoe,* which appeared in 1968. A tribute to Melville's masterpiece, the book contains some of its same dark and brooding quality.

The Dark Canoe is set in the latter half of the nineteenth century off the coast of Baja California. It is narrated by Nathan Clegg, the 16-year-old part owner, with his two older brothers, Jeremy and Caleb, of the *Alert,* a Nantucket sailing vessel in search of the wreck of the *Amy Foster,* a whaler also owned by the Cleggs. The *Amy Foster* sank in a storm in Magdalen Bay, and Caleb Clegg was stripped of his captain's license for allegedly failing to give orders to take her to the open sea where she would be in less danger of sinking during the chubasco, a fierce Pacific storm. Caleb's brother Jeremy testified against him at the hearing. When the story opens, the *Alert* is near the wreckage site, and the crew has been told of the riches in ambergris and whale oil in the wreck; however, Caleb is anxious to find the logbook, which could prove his innocence. At the very outset, we are confronted with a tantalizing mystery, for Jeremy has disappeared. Young Nathan acts as an intermediary between the crew and Caleb, a dark figure who speaks in archaic language and recites poetry from memory, holes up in his cabin on the *Alert,* and relies on Nathan to be his eyes and ears.

Nathan discovers a mysterious chest floating in the water and manages to move it to shore, where he and his confidant, Judd, steal under cover of night to scrape the barnacles from the chest, hoping eventually to open it. O'Dell prolongs these efforts perhaps a bit beyond credulity. The days are spent with the divers searching the wreck of the *Amy Foster,* the nights with Nathan and Judd laboring over the chest, which bears an uncanny resemblance to Queequeg's coffin as described in *Moby-Dick,* the book Caleb had given Nathan to read. Readers of *Moby-Dick* are meant to recognize Captain Ahab in the obsessive Caleb—perhaps even the sound of his name is meant to echo Ahab's. At one point, Caleb nails two gold doubloons, a gift from the Indians, to the mast and offers them to the man who first spots the *Amy Foster*—an unmistakable allusion to Ahab's offer to his crew in his search for the white whale. Nathan wonders at the similarity between his brother and Ahab—the scarred face, the lame leg, the obsessive temperament. However, the resemblance is only superficial, for whereas Ahab is indeed a madman, Caleb is, in fact, a wronged man and quite sane. His brother Jeremy, whom Nathan initially idolized, was, it turns out, an unscrupulous and greedy scoundrel who lied about Caleb, deliberately costing him his captain's license. Jeremy, along with Troll, who was to succeed him as captain, took a small boat one night to Isla Ballena in search of gold, but Jeremy was drowned (in peculiar circumstances to be sure) and his body recovered by Indians, who embalmed it and worshiped the blond seaman as a god.

When the ship's log is found in the wreckage, Caleb finds the vital passage that exonerates him. Then the true evil nature of Captain Troll is discovered as we learn that it was he who accompanied Jeremy on the fateful trip to the island. The greedy Troll takes off for the island himself, hoping to find the gold that Jeremy believed to be there, but Troll is conveniently killed in the attempt. The *Alert* is now left without a captain, and Nathan persuades his brother Caleb to resume that role, and, through considerable eloquence, convinces Caleb to abandon his mad vision of himself as a sort of reincarnation of Ahab. And so all is set aright. The story contains adventure and intrigue, but when all is said and done, we are left with a thin plot and perplexing theme. Caleb, the one potentially interesting character in the story, is no Ahab, as has been pointed out. Although Caleb is described as having a limp, a disfigured face, and wild, black hair, and his speech is outlandishly affected, something that alone would suggest a mental aberration, he is, in fact, one of the few genuinely decent persons in the story. He has been wronged by his brother, he cares for his reputation, and this voyage is his attempt to prove to himself that he is not mad, that he did give the appropriate command in the face of the oncoming storm that sank the *Amy Foster.* Caleb merely has a flair for the dramatic and appears to be deliberately imitating Ahab. It is Caleb who protects Nathan when Troll discovers the secret of the chest. In fact, Caleb is thrilled at the prospect of possessing what could actually be Queequeg's coffin. When it is opened, it contains only biscuits and a bottle of water, just as Queequeg's did. It also contains carvings similar to those described in *Moby-Dick,* and Caleb orders the chest prepared as a life buoy, as it is in Melville's story. Indeed, everything points to this as Queequeg's coffin, and Caleb suddenly is seized with a desire to sail the Pacific in search of the whale. But Nathan's eloquence finally prevails, and Caleb orders the coffin/life buoy cut loose. As they set sail for Nantucket, Nathan momentarily regrets having to leave Jeremy's body behind: "But if one must die, I thought, what better place to be than on a windy headland where sea-birds nest and you are worshiped as a god."[1]

One critic calls *The Dark Canoe* "an enigmatic story, made more so by its repeated allusions to Herman Melville's *Moby-Dick*" (Usrey, 283). The parallels are, as has been noted, only superficial. The book is not really a parable about the nature of evil. True, O'Dell attacks human avarice; both Jeremy and Captain Troll lose their lives because of their desire for gold. But those deaths seem only incidental to the story; indeed, Troll's death is mostly a convenience for the sake of the plot. Although excitement is generated at the outset of the story with Jeremy's disappearance and the discovery of the chest, it takes altogether too long to open that chest. And once it is opened, nothing of real significance comes of it. O'Dell seemed compelled to include this delicious mystery from one of his favorite novels but really had no con-

crete idea about what to make of it. The coffin drifts from the pages of
one novel into the pages of another and as mysteriously drifts out again.
We wonder if this perplexing appearance justifies naming the entire
book for the object. But for O'Dell the canoe, as well as all of the allusions to *Moby-Dick,* was of special significance:

> I was convinced, thinking of the story I wished to write, of the canoe's
> immortality. It lived in my mind. It therefore must live in the minds of
> others. And living, having floated Ishmael to safety, not yet finished with
> its appointed mission, where was it now? On what shores or ocean seas
> would I find it?
> What I wished to say was both simple and many-leveled. It was this:
> The stories which have been written by great writers possess lives of their
> own. They live through the years and through the centuries. They are as
> substantial as mountains, more lasting than habitations. We know the
> odes of Sappho, for instance, but under what dust heap lies the place of
> her birth?[2]

The canoe may represent O'Dell's version of Keats's Grecian urn, sug-
gesting that art possesses an immortality of its own, somehow greater
than our own individual lives. For some readers, this piggybacking of
one novel upon another does not work: "an ill-advised literary exercise,"
the *New York Times* critic groused.[3] Perhaps the error is in O'Dell's constant reference to *Moby-Dick,* reminding us of the fiction of that story
and thereby preventing us from sufficiently suspending disbelief while
we read his own tale. (The reader will recall Jean Rhys's *Wide Sargasso
Sea,* in which she builds a story on the framework of Charlotte Brontë's
Jane Eyre. Rhys, however, never shatters the illusion, never refers to the
literary work on which she is piggybacking. Thus we are allowed to
believe in both stories.) Still others find the canoe an intriguing aspect.
One writer claims that in *The Dark Canoe,* O'Dell "took metaphysical
ideas, the canoe is a life buoy is a coffin is a salvation still alive, and
framed the package for a child."[4]

Many have admired the "brooding, twilit quality which makes [*The
Dark Canoe*] an adventure more of the mind than of the sea."[5] Another
commentator calls *The Dark Canoe* a "powerful story [that] creates
splendidly the sense of suspicion after the murder, of greed and sup-
pressed mutiny on board, and Nathan's troubled realization that his
brothers are exactly the opposite of what he thought them."[6] But perhaps what readers will best recall of the book is its strangely surreal
quality. O'Dell will again capture this atmosphere, if less successfully, in

The Spanish Smile and *The Castle in the Sea,* where the lines between fantasy and reality are also disturbingly blurred.

Journey to Jericho

Journey to Jericho (1969) was O'Dell's first venture into contemporary fiction for young people, as well as one of only two books he wrote for early elementary school-age children. It is, in fact, little more than a short story and was illustrated by the noted Caldecott Award–winning artist Leonard Weisgard. This is also one of only two books for children in which O'Dell uses the third-person narrator, the other being *The Treasure of Topo-El-Bampo,* also for younger children. The story was inspired by a childhood trip O'Dell took with his mother one summer across country to visit an aunt and uncle who lived in a West Virginia coal-mining town. It seems only natural for O'Dell that he describe a journey that heads west to California. *Journey to Jericho* begins in a midwestern coal-mining community in 1965. The central figure is David Moore, a nine-year-old from a family of coal miners. David's Grandma May has just finished canning the 1,632nd jar of her prize-winning watermelon pickles, after which she vows never to make another. (She claims to have simply gotten tired of doing it.) That landmark decision is only the beginning of some great changes in David's life.

On his ninth birthday, David is very nearly killed in a mining accident, the result of his being where he should not have been. The hazards of mining are further dramatized just two days later when another, more serious, accident occurs, and David's father makes up his mind to leave mining and move to California to take up lumbering. This is a great decision for the Moore family, whose roots have long been in the coal-mining community. David's father goes on ahead to find work and get settled before sending for his family. It is a long, lonely summer without father, but at last the family receives the long-awaited envelope with three airplane tickets to California—one each for David, his mother, and his sister, Ellen.

Before they depart, Grandma May breaks her vow and makes one final jar of watermelon pickles to send to her son in California. She places the glass jar in David's hands and charges him with delivering it safely to his father. The trip across country is perhaps more exotic than we might expect one to be in 1965—they travel by airplane, train, bus, and even mule cart. All the way, David clings to the precious glass jar. When he at last sees his father in the lumber camp, David reaches out his arms with uncontainable joy, and the glass jar sails into the air, falls upon a rock, and smashes to pieces. David and his father can only look at each other and laugh.

Journey to Jericho celebrates simple virtues, the joy of family and the power of love, and close to the surface as always are O'Dell's deeply felt social concerns—the risks of mining, the difficulty of leaving one's home to settle in strange territory, the impact of economics on the family structure. But the story is too slight to effectively carry these multifaceted themes, and, after the trauma of David's brush with death in the mine at the very beginning of the story, everything else seems anticlimactic, if not inconsequential. The plot moves from a thrilling life-threatening experience to the safeguarding of a jar of pickles. O'Dell is at his best as a spinner of dramatic adventure tales—a girl surviving alone on a desert isle, a boy traveling uncharted territory with the conquistadores or grappling with a giant manta ray. However, one critic proclaims that "O'Dell has not created a more appealing and genuine male character in all his books than David Moore" (Usrey, 284). *Journey to Jericho* demonstrates O'Dell's lighter touch, and in it he captures some warm human moments.

The Treasure of Topo-El-Bampo

In 1972, O'Dell tried his hand for the second and last time at a book for children in the early elementary school years. *The Treasure of Topo-El-Bampo* is very different from *Journey to Jericho,* however. In *The Treasure,* O'Dell turns again to historical fiction, this time to eighteenth-century Mexico and the tale of the poorest village in the land, Topo-El-Bampo. The village is so poor that even the mayor, Francisco Flores, must sell his two beloved burros, Tiger and Leandro, in order to have enough to feed his wife, nine children, and Grandmother Serafina. The burros are sold to the owners of a prosperous silver mine, the Mine of the Three Brothers, the contents of which are mined and shipped around Cape Horn to Spain to finance, we are told, the king's wars. Laboring in the mine soon wears out the burros, and they are laden with silver for their final trip to the harbor at Mazatlán, where ships await to take on the silver. At Mazatlán, the burros will be driven into the sea—an easy and inexpensive way of disposing of useless beasts of burden.

On the journey, the smallest burro, Tiger, is separated from the rest and discovered by the priest of Topo-El-Bampo, Father Bruno. The priest nearly gives in to the temptation to take Tiger and the bar of sil-ver he carries back to the village. "Surely," the priest says to himself, "the Mine of the Three Brothers and the King owe us one bar. One bar, at least."[7] But the priest, a man of great social conscience who has been instrumental in saving many village men from virtual enslavement in the wretched mine, chooses the higher moral road and returns the burro to the train. However, before long the train is besieged by cutthroat bandits, and in the resulting chaos both Tiger and Leandro escape. Fol-lowing their instincts, they make their way back to Topo-El-Bampo with the bars of silver still strapped to their backs. This time the mayor and Father Bruno decide to keep the silver, which will buy food enough to last the village for many years, and "the poorest village in all of Mex-ico suddenly became the richest" (Treasure, 48).

This is a story of the evils of lust for money—a favorite theme of O'Dell's—but it is also a story of justice accomplished. In its simple, straightforward storytelling, its clearly identifiable good and evil charac-ters, and its happy ending, The Treasure of Topo-El-Bampo bears many of the traits of a folktale or allegory. The three brothers who own the silver mine are wicked, coldhearted, avaricious servants of the king. When they pray, they pray that the treasure train will safely reach the harbor, that the ships will safely reach Spain, and that the king will remember to fill their own coffers in return. The brothers are ruthless businessmen who pay their laborers no wages but give them instead food and shelter, making the miners no better off than slaves. The wealth of the three brothers and the bounty of the mine are counterpoised against the poverty of Topo-El-Bampo and its barren, rocky fields. The village of Topo-El-Bampo sits atop a hill, in contrast to the dark depths of the mine and the nearby town where the three brothers live. It is difficult not to attach moral significance to the relative locations of the village and the mine.

Among the brothers' self-serving prayers was a prayer that the king would use the silver to do God's service. Father Bruno well under-stands that, for the king of Spain, service to God means fighting wars—holy and otherwise. However, when the two innocent burros find their way back to the village, the omniscient narrator can assure us that "one of the six prayers the Vargas brothers prayed was answered" (Treasure, 48)—serving the poor is doing God's service. Thus is the village's good fortune justified and the priest relieved of any burden of guilt in accepting the silver. And any child reader will tell us that justice was served.

The monochrome illustrations by the Caldecott Award–winning artist Lynd Ward evoke the essentially somber atmosphere of the tale. O'Dell's style casts a quasi-mythical aura around the story—very similar to that of *The Black Pearl*. His characters all assume larger-than-life proportions; they seem to represent types rather than individuals. Even his settings lack specificity—Topo-El-Bampo is a poor village on a hilltop. The Mine of the Three Brothers is at the foot of a mountain, far below. The priest is good, the mayor is practical, the three brothers are evil, and the burros are pure and innocent, as saviors should be. Paul Heins refers to the book's "folkstory-like quality" and to its moving "swiftly along in uncomplicated sentences."[8] Zena Sutherland complained that the story was "overburdened by the convenience of the bandit-incident and the detailed account of the mayor's family," which she found essentially irrelevant to the core of the book.[9] For the most part, *The Treasure of Topo-El-Bampo* was received as a minor contribution from a writer still basking in the glow of a string of brilliant successes. Although O'Dell was not to do anything quite like *The Treasure* again, he would continue to be haunted by its themes, which would reappear in later, more substantial works in a variety of guises.

The Cruise of the Arctic Star

O'Dell's next published work marked a departure from fiction. *The Cruise of the Arctic Star* (1973) is impossible to categorize—part travelogue, part history, part reminiscence, part ecological treatise, but not fiction. The framework for this piece is a journey O'Dell and his second wife, Elizabeth Hall, took up the California and Oregon coasts from San Diego to the Columbia River. In his introduction, the author notes that this was the first part of a longer voyage that took them all the way to Alaska. The *Arctic Star* was a 50-foot offshore cruiser that O'Dell captained with his wife as navigator. Two hired hands completed the crew—a boisterous and unreliable character named Rod Lambert, and an inveterate fishing enthusiast, Del Boyce. The interaction among these four people provides a measure of human interest. Lambert's obnoxious ways are a constant annoyance to O'Dell, and they eventually learn that he has an unsavory reputation as a seaman. Lambert finally, and shamelessly, deserts them—but it is to O'Dell's relief. As navigator, Elizabeth is a stabilizing figure and constant source of sound advice.

Boyce is a likable character, but largely, from the standpoint of the narrative, irrelevant.

O'Dell provides a store of information about the ship, navigation, and the perils of sea travel, but the book's real interest lies in the digressions. As the ship moves up the coast, O'Dell provides, among other things, historical commentary on the landmarks they pass. He describes the Battle of San Pasqual, in which the grandiosely named Army of the West was defeated by a small band of Spanish ranchers with lances. This battle, in which the famous scout Kit Carson played a role, appears in two O'Dell novels, *Hill of the Hawk* and *Carlota*. The adventures of the famous mountain man, Jedediah Smith, occupy yet another chapter. Passing San Miguel Island, where the explorer Juan Cabrillo is buried, gives O'Dell an opportunity to recount the celebrated Spaniard's exploits. Cabrillo's remains play a key role in *The Spanish Smile*, a bizarre tale of modern California O'Dell was later to write. He almost relishes telling the tale of the greatest peacetime U.S. Navy disaster off Point Conception in 1923, when, as the result of a navigational error, seven destroyers were dashed upon the rocks and 23 men killed. Because O'Dell later met one of the navigators, he had the advantage of a firsthand point of view. O'Dell relates the story of Father Junípero Serra, founder of so many beautiful California missions, and, of course, the story of the California Gold Rush.

Into these fascinating historical vignettes, O'Dell, a California native, sprinkles some of his own personal reminiscences. At San Pedro, where his family moved when he was eight years old, he is reminded of some of his boyhood ventures. And at San Francisco, he relates the story of his first autograph signing at a San Francisco bookstore. Thirty-two people showed up, fidgeted in their seats as O'Dell talked, and in the end 15 books were sold—until one man, a kindly, eccentric millionaire, purchased the remaining stock of 85 to distribute to area hospitals, schools, prisons, and nursing homes. It was a humbling experience that O'Dell never forgot.

At every opportunity, O'Dell injects into his narrative an ecological message. A whale sighting gives him pause to lament the species' near extinction. Boyce's fishing efforts yield mercury-contaminated fish they cannot eat. O'Dell notes the rapidly disappearing brown pelican, a species being killed off with deadly insecticides that destroy its eggs. His prose begins to sparkle when he celebrates the animals. He recalls seeing the brown pelicans in the early morning:

They flew without moving their wings, in a long glide and one after the
other, along the line of the surf where the waves were just beginning to
crest, so close to the water that they were at times covered with spray,
touching the water now and again with the tips of their wings, so close
that you marveled when they did not crash. It seemed that they were not
searching for food, nor were they on their way anywhere. It was a flight
of pure joy.[10]

The sea otters, who play such an important role in *Island of the Blue Dolphins*, are becoming the victims of hunters, for whom O'Dell has little
use: "All the defenseless creatures along these shores are at the mercy of
this backward group that equates slaughter with manhood" (*Cruise*,
133). O'Dell describes a conversation with an abalone fisherman who
would like to see all the otters killed or removed because he blames
them for the diminishing numbers of abalone. O'Dell delivers a passionate defense of the otters, but he is to the fisherman a "bleeding heart."
He also deplores the harm inflicted on the dolphins by the tuna-fishing
nets. It is no accident that the book closes with the sounds of salmon
leaping on their way to their spawning grounds up the Columbia—
beautiful sounds, indeed, to O'Dell, the consummate environmentalist.

O'Dell always returns us to the narrative thread of his tale, which is
largely occupied with his troubles with Rod Lambert, the obstreperous
mate, lackadaisical of habit and loose of tongue (he takes particular joy
in devising annoying pet names for O'Dell). O'Dell quotes at length
from a work he much admires, Richard Henry Dana's *Two Years before the
Mast*, which he uses as a lesson on the importance of industry for the
derelict Lambert. Eventually Lambert deserts the ship during a brief
stopover at port, and they leave without him (although his absence is
barely felt, a comment on the quality of his work). Sometime later, Lambert contacts them by radio; he is now employed aboard another pleasure vessel, the *Island Eagle*, and he takes vengeful pleasure in a one-
sided race against the *Arctic Star*. Lambert's foolhardiness results in the
Island Eagle's running aground, and ironically Lambert becomes something of a local hero for rescuing the family aboard the ship.

The Cruise of the Arctic Star possesses the charm derived from the
author's passion for his subjects—the sea, California history, the preser-
vation of the environment. O'Dell's skills as a storyteller serve him well
here, and the first-person narrator, of which he is so fond, is ideally
suited to his purpose. This is a deeply personal book that must have
given O'Dell a great deal of pleasure to write.

The Hawk That Dare Not Hunt by Day

Scott O'Dell's widow recalls that she was once asked to interview the critic George Steiner, which prompted O'Dell to read a book of Steiner's essays. It was there that he learned of the tremendous influence that William Tyndale had on the English language.[11] He had not realized, for instance, that the translators of the King James Version of the Bible borrowed heavily from Tyndale's translation, including some of the most famous scriptural phrases. The upshot of this newfound enthusiasm was *The Hawk That Dare Not Hunt by Day*, which appeared in 1975, just after his contemporary novel, *Child of Fire* (which is discussed in chapter 7). O'Dell acknowledges his debt to Steiner by dedicating the book to him. For his return to historical fiction, O'Dell chose a European setting during the Reformation. O'Dell, as was his custom, researched this novel meticulously, even traveling the same roads through Cologne as Tyndale. (It was typical of O'Dell, an incurable traveler, to visit the places about which he wrote.) The vivid descriptions of the setting, therefore, are the result of the author's personal experiences.

The story, which covers a 12-year period from 1524 to 1536, is divided into five books, recalling the five-act plays of Renaissance drama. The narrator is Tom Barton, a seaman working, at the book's opening, on the *Black Pearl,* a ship belonging to his uncle Jack, who makes much of his money smuggling. Currently, Uncle Jack is smuggling into London copies of Martin Luther's latest manifesto, and he sends young Tom off to find William Tyndale, who is a prospective buyer. Tom finds Tyndale, is immediately taken with the man's spiritual qualities, and offers him passage on the *Black Pearl* to the continent, where Tyndale hopes to find a printer for his translation of the Bible. Tom gets Tyndale safely to Hamburg, and Tyndale teaches Tom to read in the process. One of the seamen recently hired is a dangerous fanatic named Belsey who is bent on capturing Tyndale. Belsey attempts a mutiny, but thanks to Tom it fails, and Belsey goes overboard. Thus ends the first book.

The second book resumes the story the following summer as the *Black Pearl* sails up the Rhine to Antwerp, where Tom departs for Cologne to find Tyndale, whose devoted follower he has become. Several chapters depict the religious turmoil in the southern German states as Tyndale is forced to flee Cologne. In the midst of all this, Belsey, who did not die in the mutiny after all, turns up again and discloses to Tom the fact that the *Black Pearl* was actually willed to Tom by his late father and

that Uncle Jack has unlawfully acquired it. Of course, Tom has reason to
doubt Belsey's word as well as his motives, and he stores this information in the back of his mind for the time being.

The third book begins several months later as the New Testament
translation is completed and readied for shipment to England. They
deliver the books to London, at which time Tom finally confronts his uncle
regarding his father's will. Uncle Jack maintains there was none, and the
subject is dropped. When they reach their home, they find Belsey and the
king's officers waiting, and they are arrested under suspicion of smuggling. Uncle Jack lands in Clink prison—the most deplorable of London's prisons, usually reserved for only the most hardened criminals.
Belsey allows Tom to go free, however, in return for part interest in the
Black Pearl. Tom has little choice but to cooperate with the unscrupulous
Belsey, and they form a trading company with Tom and Belsey each
holding one-third and one-third being sold to a dandy named Henry
Phillips.

In the fourth book, the plague strikes and Uncle Jack dies in Clink
prison—he will remain a mysterious figure. The truth about the will is
never discovered. Tom finds a new friend in Ed Groat, a shipmate, and,
on an expedition to Venice by way of Spain, he takes on Juan de Palos—
who sailed with Christopher Columbus. (This is probably the greatest
stretch of historical fact in the book, which is on the whole quite faithful to history.) The evidence becomes overwhelming that Belsey and
Phillips are after Tyndale, that they have been in the employ of Henry
VIII and in contact with the Holy Roman Emperor Charles V, both of
whom want Tyndale tried for heresy. Phillips's true colors are finally
revealed as he betrays Tyndale into the hands of his enemies.

The fifth and last book opens with Tom conceiving a plot to get Tyndale out of jail, but Tyndale refuses to cooperate, fearing that someone
may be hurt. Tom even has an audience with Henry VIII, beseeching his
help—an interesting commentary on how fickle the political climate
can be. Henry, originally an enemy of Tyndale, has a change of heart
when he divorces his Catholic wife, Catherine of Aragon (the niece of
Charles V), and marries the Protestant Anne Boleyn. But, of course,
Henry now has no influence with Charles. Tyndale is tried and found
guilty, and Tom witnesses his hanging and burning.

Tom, with the help of Juan de Palos and Ed Groat, tracks down
Phillips (Belsey has died of the plague and therefore gotten his just
deserts). But Tom, seeing the pathetic Phillips in rags in a sleazy tavern

in Antwerp, finds that he cannot kill him. Instead, he gives him a few coins and departs, deciding that that is what Tyndale would have done. And so the story ends with Tom's forgiving his great enemy. The story is convoluted and loose ends remain, but it is filled with colorful characters and intrigue, and O'Dell depicts an almost panoramic sweep of Reformation Europe. One critic waxed enthusiastically that *"The Hawk That Dare Not Hunt by Day* is as good as any historical novel O'Dell has written."* Particularly credited are the "gripping plot," the characterization, and the historical accuracy (Usrey, 286). As with most of O'Dell's historical fiction, *Hawk* includes its share of avarice, wickedness, and violence. From kings to peasants, people can be cruel and heartless. Danger stalks the country fields and crowded city streets. And honor is a rare commodity. But, also true to O'Dell's view of the world, honor is not entirely absent. Good people do live among us, and as often as not good does triumph in the end. The world is filled with evil—O'Dell is too honest a writer to tell us otherwise—but he never leaves us without hope. His ultimate message is that we must forgive our enemies if we ourselves are to find peace of mind. This is the lesson learned by Karana and a host of other O'Dell protagonists.

Hawk has been out of print in its original form for some time—the books with European subjects have not had the same staying power as those with American subjects. However, Bob Jones University Press published a bowdlerized version of *Hawk,* omitting the references to drinking, gambling, smuggling, and other unsavory activities. O'Dell himself agreed to this arrangement, apparently believing it was better to have a sanitized version in print than none at all.

Conclusion

Between *The Cruise of the Arctic Star* and *The Hawk That Dare Not Hunt by Day,* O'Dell published his first contemporary novel for adolescents, *Child of Fire.* He would eventually write six contemporary stories for that age group, although none achieved the acclaim of his historical fiction. The experiments of the 1970s were largely sporadic forays that failed to reap the success to which O'Dell had become accustomed. Of all the works of this period, *The Hawk That Dare Not Hunt by Day* is probably his best, the other books seeming slight by comparison. O'Dell undoubtedly discovered that his strength was historical fiction, that he was not especially suited to storytelling for younger children, and that literature, for him, implied a moral obligation. Following *Hawk* he turned again to the Old Southwest and produced five more historical novels out of that setting, including one of his most ambitious writing projects, the Seven Serpents Trilogy. O'Dell's experimentation brought him back to where he began—the historical novel of the American Southwest and of Spanish America.

Chapter Six
The Seven Serpents Trilogy

All journeys worth making are dangerous.

—O'Dell, *The Feathered Serpent* (1981)

In 1979, O'Dell published the first of three books dealing with the adventures of a young Jesuit in the New World. *The Captive* recounts Julián Escobar's encounter with the declining Mayan civilization. *The Feathered Serpent,* which appeared in 1981, resumes the tale and describes Julián's journey to the Aztec capital, Moctezuma's Tenochtitlán, just prior to the arrival of Cortés. *The Amethyst Ring* (1983) concludes the cycle, recounting Julián's travels with Pizarro to the empire of the Incas, the resulting conquest, and ultimately his return to his native Spain. The stories are as far-fetched as this brief synopsis sounds, but they do not want for adventure, and they are filled with fascinating details about these three great American civilizations. O'Dell was fascinated by the early Native American civilizations, and he reported that he took no fewer than three journeys to Central and South America before he wrote the trilogy:

> When you tramp around in the Cloud Cities of Cuzco and Machu Picchu, three miles high in the Peruvian Andes, and your feet are lumps of lead and your breath comes in gasps, you live these details as you write. To give your work more life you descend three miles to the miasmic headwaters of the Amazon, home of the Head Hunters, to get the feel of the vast country the conquistadors conquered. ("History," 34)

It is easy to see why one of the hallmarks of O'Dell's fiction is the compelling setting and atmosphere he creates.

The Captive

The narrator and central figure of the trilogy is Julián Escobar, a seminarian who joins a Spanish nobleman, Don Luis de Arroyo, on a trip to the New World, where Don Luis wishes to exploit the land and people.

Julián, on the other hand, naively wishes only to save souls. *The Captive* begins with a sea voyage, by now virtually a commonplace in O'Dell's novels. The ship, the *Santa Margarita*, becomes almost a character itself, playing a key role in all three books. On the voyage, Julián learns that Don Luis plans to enter the slave trade, to which Julián is vehemently opposed, but about which he can do little. The *Santa Margarita* reaches an island the Spaniards call Isla Arroyo after their home in Spain. One of the crew, an ex-convict named Guzmán, is swept away by tales of gold in the New World and quickly becomes the embodiment of Spanish greed.

On the island live friendly Indians whom Julián hopes to convert, but he is troubled that he has not completed seminary and, insisting he is not a priest, he refuses Don Luis's request to bless the Indians. Julián quickly earns the trust of the Indians, who invite him to their village, little more than a collection of ramshackle huts with a carved idol whose fierce appearance seems, to Julián, to contradict the gentle nature of the Indians. Of course, Julián is blind to the fact that his stories of a loving savior seem to be contradicted by the avaricious and ruthless behavior of the Spaniards. When a vein of gold is discovered, Guzmán organizes the Indians to help mine it. The haul is so great that Don Luis renames the island Isla Del Oro—Island of Gold (a name that O'Dell will resurrect in his contemporary tale *The Spanish Smile*). A complicated series of events turns the Indians against the greedy Spaniards, and Don Luis, unable to establish a legal title to the island (the governor has already given it to his brother-in-law), decides to flee with as much gold as his ship will carry. The ship sinks in a hurricane, with Julián and a stallion named Bravo as the only apparent survivors.

Julián finds himself on another island, and Crusoe-like he fends for himself, salvaging what he can from the wreck. In these "survival" chapters, Julián builds a hut of lava rocks and mud, learns to ride Bravo, makes shoes and clothes, and brings fire for himself from the island's active volcano, which he names St. John the Baptist. He soon discovers that he is being watched by a young girl, a Mayan named Ceela, from whom he learns the Mayan language (Julián is adept at languages, a skill that opens many doors for him). While he is trying to teach Ceela about Christianity, she teaches him about Kukulcán, the Feathered Serpent, a fair-haired, fair-skinned Mayan god who sailed away centuries ago leaving only a promise to return sometime in the future. In an arrogant attempt to rid the islanders of their heathen ways, Julián blows up the Mayan idol, using gunpowder salvaged from the *Santa Margarita*.

Ironically, the explosion that was to rid him of the pagan presence brings out from hiding a Spanish dwarf, Guillermo Cantú, survivor of a previous shipwreck, who will be the source of much grief for Julián. Cantú had been spared by the Maya because they revered dwarfs, and he knows how to use to his advantage the Mayan superstitions. Cantú, an enigmatic figure, at once appealing and repulsive, is to become a key figure in all three books. The clever and devious dwarf hatches a plot whereby Julián would impersonate the god Kukulcán and thus bring honor and riches to both Julián and himself. Julián agrees to this dangerous scheme in part because Cantú threatens to have him sacrificed if he will not. Additionally, Cantú informs Julián that the capital of the island, the City of the Seven Serpents, is in imminent danger of an attack from a greedy Spaniard named Don Luis de Arroyo—he has survived the hurricane after all. It is puzzling that a would-be priest who resorted to gunpowder to blow up an offending pagan idol could be so easily persuaded to impersonate another pagan deity for very dubious reasons. The ruse, nevertheless, is successful. When Julián enters the City of the Seven Serpents on horseback preceded by a well-placed gunpowder explosion, it is enough to persuade most of the populace and two of the three chief priests. To his great horror, the first act Julián witnesses in his name is a human sacrifice, in which a priest cuts open the chest of the living victim and wrenches out the still-beating heart, lifting it up for all to see. Thus the story ends, and we are left with the image of the crafty dwarf, Cantú, smiling in the wings.

O'Dell is indulging his fascination with Native American cultures in this and in the sequels. For example, Julián relates how, on the Isla Del Oro, he observed Ayo, the chieftain or cacique,

> as he went down the trail that led to the lagoon. He walked as if he had reverence for the earth he trod upon, for the trees he passed and the running water. He stopped to pick a wildflower and place it in his hair. His people, as I had observed them in the few days I had been on the island, were much like him—gentle, courteous to each other, given to laughter whenever there was the least thing to laugh about.[1]

At the same time Julián is perplexed at how these happy people could have conceived such a horrible god as the monstrous, three-headed figure with blue hair and "uneven rows of blood-red teeth" (*Captive*, 42). O'Dell enjoys providing the reader with factual details of Mayan culture—the fact, for example, that Mayans traditionally flattened their children's foreheads by fastening boards to them, and that they deliberately crossed their children's eyes by forcing infants to stare at a pebble suspended from a string. And, of course, we learn a great deal about their religion. For many reviewers, the historical information was the strongest feature of the book. Some admired the characterizations, and one found "Julián's transformation from insecure, human seminarian to pretend god . . . remarkable in its honest development."[2] Another reviewer noted that

> It is a measure of [O'Dell's] seriousness and his skill that the suspense focuses not on events, which have so far been swift and stunning, inevitable and unexpected, or on the artfully foreshadowed intrigue, confrontations, and dangers that are sure to follow, but on Julián's moral choices and on what he will make of his false, exalted position.[3]

John Warren Stewig admired *The Captive* for its style: its careful foreshadowing of events, its vivid imagery, its repetition for the sake of emphasis, its use of syntax for variety and to establish character, and its effective descriptions of setting, character, and social milieu.[4]

Certainly the story does not lack for adventure, and, true, Julián is confronted with what should be some difficult moral choices. But we see or hear very little of the spiritual torment that should affect a seminarian who was a follower of the antislavery priest Bartolomé de las Casas. Julián's turnabout seems all too convenient and his willingness to be used by Cantú in an elaborate deception may make for some exciting fiction, but it does little to establish a convincing character. This sentiment was expressed in one of the most famous reviews of *The Captive,* that written by Leon Garfield, himself a distinguished author of historical novels for young people. Garfield criticized O'Dell's refusal to become involved in his characters: "At no time are we really with the hero. We receive no impression of his sensations. There are none of those touches that enliven the imagination. When our hero's hands are bound behind his back, there seems to be no reaction, no sense of helplessness, of indignity." In summary, Garfield writes that *The Captive* lacks that "shaft of imagination that illuminates the narrative and makes it live."[5]

The Feathered Serpent

The cliff-hanging conclusion of *The Captive* would leave readers in the lurch for two years, for its sequel, *The Feathered Serpent,* did not appear until after O'Dell's tale of the American Revolution, *Sarah Bishop* (1980). *The Feathered Serpent,* like a new episode in a prime-time soap opera, resumes at virtually the very moment that *The Captive* had concluded. O'Dell reiterates the gruesome, but historically accurate, details of the human sacrifice. Julián at once senses the hatred and suspicion of Chalco, the high priest, who will remain his nemesis, but for the time being, Julián is hailed as a god and virtual ruler of the city. Julián uses his newfound power to begin restoring the dilapidated City of the Seven Serpents, takes up residence in the ruined palace, and, remarkably, finds a forgotten library of Mayan history, a transparent device used to educate the reader about Mayan history. Julián at first desires to bring Christianity to the Mayans, but his efforts are sidetracked by the imminent attack of Don Luis. Then he decides to raise the *Santa Margarita.* Raising the ship is important to Julián and Cantú for two reasons—it contains cannon that can be used to defend the city and, perhaps more important to Cantú, it contains all the gold mined by Don Luis's men while on the Isla Del Oro. But the ship lies in three fathoms of water, and the accomplishment of this feat tests the reader's credulity.

Equally incredible is the skillful attack Julián orchestrates against the city of Tikan, which is ruled by Don Luis. Julián's knowledge of warfare comes from his reading of Julius Caesar's *Gallic Wars.* In fact, most of his knowledge comes from what he has read. After the battle he follows the dubious example of Nero—keep the populace entertained to distract them from their worries. And from Marcus Aurelius, he takes this advice: "That which doth not hurt the city itself . . . cannot hurt any of its citizens."[6] His success as a warrior, however, must be largely attributed to his disguise as Kukulcán, which brings the Mayans of Tikan to their knees. Don Luis is now Julián's prisoner. Julián is confronted with demands for 50 human sacrifices to celebrate the victory, and he acquiesces to permit 10, as if reducing the number of victims would mollify the deed. Again, the anguish and the soul-searching we might rightly expect from his facing such a choice are just not apparent.

Julián, inspired by his conquest and intoxicated by the prospect of an empire of his own, next immerses himself in rebuilding his city. He is behaving more like an enlightened despot than a man of God. Julián's corruption is not entirely explained and is one of the more troubling aspects of the trilogy. Whereas we might expect him to be building churches and schools, he is restoring pagan temples and palaces. To further his enterprises, he feels he must conquer another city to obtain workers. But first, he decides to journey to the land of the Aztec emperor

Moctezuma II and his magnificent city of Tenochtitlán, where he hopes to learn something about governance. Julián is so dazzled by the display of wealth and power in Tenochtitlán that he is inspired to make his own city even more splendid. His corruption has become almost complete. However, before they leave Moctezuma's city, Julián and the dwarf are captured by the Spaniards under the leadership of Hernán Cortés and impressed into the service of the Spanish king. Here they learn of the plans to sack Tenochtitlán for its gold. Here also they meet two familiar faces, the Mayan girl Ceela, who had befriended Julián on the beach after the wreck of the *Santa Margarita,* and Don Luis. Ceela has now fully converted to Christianity and goes by the name of Dona Marina. Don Luis has escaped from captivity in Tikan. Despite Julián's best efforts to warn Moctezuma, he falls prey to his own trusting nature and the insatiable greed of the Spaniards. Moctezuma is fatally wounded by one of his own subjects, who sees him as a traitor and coward, and, in the resulting confusion, the Spaniards sack the city. The outnumbered Spaniards are eventually defeated, although Cortés escapes with a few men. Don Luis, on the other hand, is captured and becomes a ritual sacrifice at the hands of Aztec priests. The story concludes with Julián and Cantú pursuing the high priest Chalco, who had also been in Tenochtitlán, back to the City of the Seven Serpents, where Julián hopes to reprise his performance as Kukulcán.

Unlike *The Captive,* in which Julián played a reasonably credible role, *The Feathered Serpent* seems merely an excuse for O'Dell to describe the Aztec civilization and the fall of Moctezuma. The novel's greatest weakness is its main character, Julián, who seemingly must become all things to all people. Equally at home with Cortés and with Moctezuma, a seminarian who had no further aspirations than to save the souls of Indians now becomes a skilled strategist in war and an effective administrator of government. Moreover, for so remarkable a personality as he must have been, we learn very little of him. As one reviewer put it, "[H]e displays odd vacancies of personality. He seems to have little emotional life, no real curiosity about an alien society and (strangest of all) an implausible lack of awareness of the opposite sex."[7] O'Dell defended the lack of sexual awareness in the novels thus: "Julián Escobar was a seminarian living in an age whose energies were not absorbed by sex, in contrast to the present when the phenomena dependent upon the differences between the male and the female are presented to us on a twenty-four-hour schedule, a bacchanalia beginning with children as they eat their Wheaties and ending only with those who cannot sleep."[8]

The Amethyst Ring

Picking up where *The Feathered Serpent* left off, *The Amethyst Ring* takes Julián from the City of the Seven Serpents to Peru and the Inca empire, and then finally back to his home in Spain. After witnessing the collapse of the Aztec empire, Julián and Cantú return home to find another ship in their harbor. The ship, named the *Delfín Azul* (which means "blue dolphin"—O'Dell never hesitated to recycle a favorite name) has been seized by the Mayans, led by Chalco, the duplicitous high priest who had returned to the city ahead of Julián and persuaded the people that their god was dead. Among those spared from the *Delfín Azul* is a Spanish bishop named Pedroza who has harsh words for Julián and what he has done. Julián's former desire to be a Catholic priest is rekindled, and he repeatedly asks the bishop to consecrate him, but Pedroza refuses.

The conflict between Julián and Chalco escalates as they attempt to fortify the city against Cortés's expected attack. At one point, Julián exclaims in the presence of Cantú, "Will no one rid me of this upstart priest?"[9] which echoes Henry II's remark about Thomas á Becket—a reference not lost on Cantú. To be sure, most of O'Dell's youthful readers may not catch the allusion, but it is to O'Dell's credit that he never condescends to his readers. While Julián is away seeking help from a neighboring city, the dwarf kills Chalco, believing it to be Julián's wish. According to custom, human sacrifices are made at Chalco's funeral, and Julián forces the bishop to attend. Exasperated at the bishop's stubbornness in refusing to make him a priest, Julián himself gives the order for the bishop to be sacrificed. Julián removes the bishop's amethyst ring from his finger. This is, perhaps, one of the most difficult episodes to accept in the entire trilogy. Most of the Spaniards are ruthless and avaricious, but Pedroza was a man of faith, whose greatest sin was his implacable belief that the Indians were soulless savages. That he should be subjected to the bloody sacrifice for refusing to grant Julián's selfish request for ordination seems extreme to say the least. And Julián's audacity in removing the bishop's ring seems beyond redemption. Julián's defense is that Pedroza was "stubborn, truculent, and vain, a man so steeped in himself that he couldn't tell the love of ritual from love itself" (*Amethyst,* 65). Not all readers will buy that defense, but the sentiment is another example of O'Dell's distaste for the hypocrisy of religious institutions.

To make matters worse, Cantú, never to be trusted, deserts the city under cover of night in the *Santa Margarita,* with her cannon, men, and

gold. Cortés arrives and sends Dona Marina (the former Ceela) to persuade Julián to surrender. Now, as a Christian convert, she chastises
Julián for not stopping the blood sacrifices. At last he is taken prisoner
by Cortés, but Dona Marina arranges for his escape. He lands once
again on a deserted beach and must make use of his survival skills. By
this time, Julián has reflected on his failure in the City of the Seven Serpents, on his greed and lust for power, and when the opportunity arises
again for him to assume leadership of a small Indian community, he
refuses.

His adventures take him to Central America where he goes into business, first with a woman who weaves hats and then with a more ambitious trader, Tzom Zambac, who deals in gorgeous cloaks of feathers.
But Cortés has put a price on Julián's head, and he must flee further
south to Panamá, where he meets Francisco Pizarro and joins his expedition to Peru—this time unabashedly for the gold. Julián quickly learns
the Incan tongue (too quickly many readers are likely to feel) and
becomes the chief translator for Pizarro and the Incan ruler Atahualpa.
Pizarro is a braggart and a bully who insults and then takes prisoner the
great Atahualpa. Perhaps in response to those critics who wondered why
Julián never fell in love, O'Dell introduces Atahualpa's favorite daughter, Chima, with whom Julián becomes infatuated. Unfortunately, their
romance is cut short when her father is tried and mercilessly executed
on a trumped-up charge. Julián himself, who has been charged by
Valverde, a priest accompanying Pizarro, with killing Bishop Pedroza,
must flee in the confusion following Atahualpa's death.

Crossing the Andes to Cuzco, he searches for Chima and finds his
way to an Incan convent where he believes she is residing. There he is
seduced by the priestess of the convent—his first sexual experience—
and they have an affair that lasts several months, until her former lover
returns in the spring. Only then does he find Chima, who rebuffs him—
the final straw for Julián. He makes his way back to Spain, where
Cantú, now a wealthy nobleman, shares some of the treasure with him.
But Julián gives his portion to the Brothers of the Poor and deposits the
amethyst ring, the last vestige of his old self, in the poor box at the
church, and the story ends with his ringing the bell on a rusty chain at
the humble dwelling of the Brothers of the Poor, giving up both his
dream of becoming a priest and his fabulous wealth.

These perhaps overly long summaries will indicate the major
strengths and weaknesses of the trilogy. O'Dell wanted to describe the
fall of the Aztec and Inca empires as well as include information on

Mayan culture, and he boldly attempted to weave them into a unified story with a central character. Consequently, he has created a protagonist of extraordinary range and incredible facility, who turns out to be neither believable nor sympathetic. The books do succeed in conveying an exciting historical perspective about one of the most compelling—and tragic—periods in the history of Central and South America and could very well inspire young readers to explore these great civilizations further.

The enthusiasm some early reviewers displayed for the trilogy has not been sustained. In retrospect, the books do not measure up to the works of O'Dell's golden years of the 1960s and early 1970s. Julián is a thinly drawn character, with unconvincing motivation and virtually nonexistent emotions. The other characters appear and reappear so often and in so many different places that the setting has an almost small-town atmosphere where everyone knows everybody. One critic writes, "As historical fiction, the trilogy is a failure; its main appeal lies in its dramatic and sensational presentation of the downfall of two great civilizations. Ultimately, the reader knows the civilizations will fall, and how and why. But, from O'Dell's trilogy, the reader does not know how it felt to be either the conquerors or the conquered" (Usrey, 291)

These flaws aside, O'Dell should not be denied his due for his insistence on treating serious themes in books for young people. The dominant themes are familiar O'Dell concerns. He expresses sympathy for the ill-fated Native Americans and contempt for the rapacious Europeans. The Spaniards are depicted as cruel, shameless, and greedy—albeit their malice is quite democratic, for they can be equally as treacherous to each other as to the Indians. Another important theme in the trilogy is O'Dell's skepticism of religious institutions. The two Roman Catholic priests who appear in the story are self-righteous, inflexible, and intolerant of the Indians. This skepticism, however, extends beyond the institution of the Christian Church. O'Dell's harshest criticism of the Indians is reserved for their religious institutions, and the priests are the least trustworthy people in the City of the Seven Serpents. But this disdain for the institution of religion should not be confused with a disdain for religion. What Julián finally comes to realize is that he needs not the trappings of priestly office, but the humble spirit of the truly holy person as found in the ramshackle establishment of the Brothers of the Poor.

Throughout the trilogy, generally speaking, the art is overpowered by O'Dell's didactic messages. Too often we suspect that the plot and characters are being manipulated to satisfy his moral or hortative purpose. When O'Dell wrote of his experiences creating this trilogy, he recognized some of the problems it posed—"A historical trilogy for the young is a well-nigh untameable beast. The momentum gained in the first book tends to be progressively lost as the story moves on into the second book and then into the third." But he defends his work in a superb rationale for the entire subgenre of historical novels:

> [T]he historical novel, whether in three parts or one, despite all of its technical difficulties and in the face of neglect from young readers, is still worth the writer's best. Children tend to believe that they have come into the world full-blown, thunderbolts directly from the forehead of Jove. It is good for children to think that they are unique, as different from one another as are their thumb prints. But it is not good to think that their problems are unique. People before them had problems to solve—many of the same problems, or related ones, by which children are now bedeviled. ("Tribulations," 144)

Chapter Seven

When the Past Meets the Present

Caught between two worlds . . .

—O'Dell, *Black Star, Bright Dawn* (1988)

Scott O'Dell first experimented with contemporary fiction for children in the late 1960s with his brief tale *Journey to Jericho,* aimed at very young readers. He was eventually to write six novels with contemporary settings for adolescent readers. The first two, *Child of Fire* and *Kathleen, Please Come Home,* appeared in 1974 and 1978 respectively. They are both versions of the problem novel so popular at that time. In the early 1980s, while O'Dell was still working on the Seven Serpents Trilogy, he decided to return again to contemporary fiction. But this time he attempted something wildly different from anything he had tried before—the result nearly defies categorization, but the term Gothic fiction comes closest to capturing the flavor of *The Spanish Smile* (1982) and *The Castle in the Sea* (1983). For reasons that will become apparent, O'Dell did not pursue this strand of fiction further, but he did write two more contemporary stories, taking as his settings two regions he had not tackled before—the Gulf Coast of Florida in *Alexandra* (1984) and Alaska in *Black Star, Bright Dawn* (1988). In all four of these novels, O'Dell draws heavily on his interests in historical culture and its impact on our lives today. And in all cases, he sees a conflict between the cultural traditions of the past, for which he reveals tremendous respect, and the ways of modern society, which he typically sees as crass, materialistic, and increasingly insensitive.

Child of Fire

Child of Fire (1974) is the story of a young Hispanic (O'Dell uses the then-current term *Chicano*) boy, a high school dropout, who attempts against great odds to rise from poverty and make his imprint on the world. The narrator is a juvenile parole officer named Delaney, an unusual choice for a book for young readers, but more of that later. The tale is set near San Diego, close to the Mexican-American border in territory that O'Dell knew well.

The novel opens at a bullfight in Mexico where Delaney is looking for one of his charges, Ernest Sierra. The bullfight takes three chapters to describe and ends climactically when a 16-year-old named Manuel Castillo jumps into the ring in the face of the charging bull, disrupts the fight, and inadvertently causes the bullfighter to be gored. As it turns out, Manuel is the leader of a Chicano gang, the Conquistadores, and Ernie Sierra is the leader of a rival gang, the Owls. Both boys are enamored of the same flirtatious waitress, whom Manuel's foolhardy act was intended to impress.

Delaney, who has been demoted to the juvenile parole division for carelessly allowing a prisoner to escape, takes a special interest in Manuel, whom he believes to be essentially good and honest. Through Delaney's intervention, Manuel is persuaded to return to school, and for a time the community knows peace. Things begin to turn sour when Delaney accepts the gangs' invitation to a cockfight—across the border in Mexico, where the authorities are more lax. The brutality of the cockfight is described in even more grisly detail than the bullfight. Manuel is a reckless gambler, but he wins big and in the grand finale, his prized cock defeats Ernie Sierra's. But Ernie's defeat is not taken lightly, and immediately after the cockfight the Conquistadores' horses are discovered dead at the bottom of a cliff, having been driven maliciously over the edge. The Owls are suspected, naturally, but nothing can be proven.

The action escalates when Delaney arrests Ernie on suspicion of drug trafficking and, in a subsequent shootout, Manuel kills Ernie's shady cousin, Paco, saving Delaney's life in the process. But Manuel's heroics come to nothing, and before long he drops out of school and signs on with a Panamanian tuna boat. Through secondhand information, Delaney learns about more of Manuel's adventures: he leads a mutiny on the tuna boat when he discovers it is an illegal operation; he escapes from a South American prison in a garbage can; and he finally ends up on the high seas. In the meantime, back home, the local grape vineyard owner, who employs many of the Hispanics in the community, is purchasing an automated grape picker, which will likely put most of them out of work. And who should come to their rescue but Manuel, now fully matured and ready to direct his leadership abilities to positive use, championing the workers' cause against the vineyard owner. One commentator has sardonically noted that "there is no evidence that [Manuel's] agricultural background extends beyond the nurture of an occasional marijuana plant, but he quickly becomes a natural leader, a 16-year-old Cesar Chavez."[1] The day comes when the automatic picker is to be put into use, and the workers look helplessly on—until Manuel boldly kneels in the path of the machine—reminiscent, of course, of his stance in the path of the charging bull at the story's beginning. This time, however, the result is tragic: he is mangled and killed.

His death is described as an accident in the local newspaper, which also happens to be owned by the proprietor of the vineyard, and, we presume, the workers' cause is lost. As for Delaney, his reputation is restored, and he is offered a regular officer's job on the force again. He declines, believing now, with his wife, that "it's better to keep people from being arrested than it is to spend your time arresting people."[2]

Manuel is a hero of potentially tragic proportions, a complex figure whom O'Dell attempts to portray as larger than life. His economic and social circumstances seem to doom him from the beginning. It is true that some of his misfortune can be attributed to his youth and impetuosity. He had hoped, by his actions at the bullfight, to impress a girl, but he eventually finds that she is callow, insincere, and even malicious—a stereotype to which many readers have objected. In the vineyard, his valor results in his own death, and we have little assurance that the lot of vineyard workers will be any better because of it. He is the child of fire—impetuous, unyielding, and inevitably consumed by his own passionate nature.

Despite this multifaceted and seemingly vibrant plot, the book often seems to plod along, bogged down in the minutiae of daily living. The first four-fifths of the book is slow in development with the focus too often on the narrator, Delaney, and too seldom on Manuel. And the last fifth of the book unfolds too swiftly to do justice to the dramatic events it tries to describe. Some of the gritty experiences that ultimately give Manuel his strongly principled character happen offstage as in a Greek tragedy—in a South American prison, on the high seas, and elsewhere. Readers might be more engaged if they were allowed to witness these events firsthand.

As social commentary, the novel has some significant shortcomings. O'Dell depicts the plight of the rural Hispanic poor, but chooses to sidestep the reasons behind it. He is curiously reluctant to point an accusing finger at the dominant white culture. Part of this fault may be due to the narrator's being a white policeman. And Delaney does reveal a patronizing attitude toward the Hispanic youths. At one point he remarks, "Chicanos are good mechanics" (*Child,* 63), a foolish and blatantly racist remark. He also elaborates on the concept of *machismo,* comparing it to the medieval concept of chivalry: "The knight courted a lady and fought for her. If he won her, it was the highest happiness. The *machista* fights for a woman against another man. But in this fight the woman is only an excuse. She is not important. It is the defeat of the rival that's important" (*Child,* 42). According to Delaney, the chivalric ideal has degenerated into senseless violence. But what has wrought this transformation—social, political, and economic upheaval—is never adequately broached. It is strongly implied that lack of parental guidance is a source of the problem—father figures are virtually absent throughout the book. And, at the conclusion, O'Dell hints that the white exploitation of the Hispanics may be the source of their economic woes. The automated grape picker suggests that there might be still further impoverishment among the Hispanic population, but are we not to wonder why the living conditions were so deplorable prior to the machine's arrival? This novel leaves us with the nagging feeling that there is another story that needs to be told.

A final problem is that of Delaney as the narrator. It is unusual for an adolescent novel to have an adult as the first-person narrator. It seems unlikely that an adult—and a parole officer to boot—would ever be an engaging or credible narrative voice for a teenage audience. More disturbing is that at the novel's conclusion Delaney has center stage. Manuel has given his life for a lost cause, and the only redemption we are offered is that Delaney, his reputation once again intact, has chosen to remain in juvenile parole work in the hope of saving other young people. This may be slight consolation for the teenage reader whose interest lies in the plight of the Hispanic youths.

Child of Fire received both high praise and sharp criticism—praise as a "contemporary parable . . . with a self-contained dignity" and criticism for its patronizing and inaccurate representation of Hispanic culture.[3] Paul Heins objected to "the offhand manner of the style [which] only adds to the banality of the story."[4] Indeed, the inaccurate and condescending portrayal of Hispanic culture is likely to be the most disturbing aspect of this novel for informed readers. And for uninformed readers, it could be the most damaging aspect. For example, O'Dell suggests that Manuel's lineage goes back to Spain, an inaccuracy that, it has been pointed out, would be offensive to Hispanics (Senick, 170).

Despite these shortcomings, the story contains some fascinating features. The descriptions of the bullfight and the cockfight are carefully detailed and reveal O'Dell's misgivings over brutality to animals. And it has been pointed out that the cockfight bears a striking resemblance to gang warfare: the cocks are bred to kill, and the young Chicano gang members seem to have a similar violence bred into their veins—so much so that it seems to be their only purpose for existing (Usrey, 285). Finally, there is no question that O'Dell's sympathy lies with the Hispanic youths and the difficulty they have living, as it were, between two cultures. They are all children of fire, too swiftly consumed by their uncontrolled passion. The message is a profoundly important one.

Kathleen, Please Come Home

Four years after *Child of Fire*, O'Dell returned again to a contemporary setting in *Kathleen, Please Come Home* (1978). (In the intervening years he had written three more historical novels, *The Hawk That Dare Not Hunt by Day*, *Zia*, and *Carlota*.) *Kathleen, Please Come Home* is unique among O'Dell's works in that it employs two first-person narrators, with the narrative divided into three parts—the first and third contain the diary entries of Kathleen, a troubled teenager, and the middle part represents her mother's diary.

The story opens on 1 January as Kathleen Winters, an apparently typical 15-year-old living with her widowed mother, an English teacher, begins writing in her new diary. On 3 January she meets a new student at school, Sybil Langley, a wealthy, self-indulgent teen unencumbered by moral values. Sybil uses every drug imaginable—marijuana, hashish, PCP, heroin, angel dust, and pills. Kathleen's first assessment of Sybil— "I liked Sybil right off"—suggests that she is both immature and a poor judge of character. On 28 January, under Sybil's influence, Kathleen takes her first drink of liquor, and on 12 February she smokes her first marijuana cigarette. Kathleen's descent to perdition is taking place with remarkable speed. It is also on 12 February that she meets Ramón Sandoval, an illegal immigrant with whom she falls in love. Ramón opposes Kathleen's use of drugs, but Sybil proves to be a more powerful force. Kathleen and Ramón soon find themselves in a passionate relationship, and, in the spring, Kathleen announces to her mother that she and Ramón are engaged to be married. One commentator describes this as O'Dell's portrayal of "the euphoria and total commitment of first love."[5] Mrs. Winters maintains a valiant composure in the face of her daughter's unsettling plans. But, eventually, unable to restrain herself any longer, she reports Ramón to the authorities, and he is forced to flee.

During his flight, Ramón is shot and killed in an ambush. When Kathleen learns of her mother's betrayal, she runs away from home—and thus ends the first part.

Part II picks up the narrative where Part I leaves off, but the point of view shifts to Mrs. Winters—it is now her diary we are reading. We see her distress as she gradually realizes that Kathleen has run away from home, and we see her desperate attempts to reach her daughter. After offering a reward for information leading to Kathleen, Mrs. Winters is led to a sleazy Tijuana bar where she does spot Kathleen briefly, but her daughter avoids her. Most readers will be glad for Part III and the return to Kathleen's diary to discover just what has been happening to her.

In Part III we learn that Kathleen has run off with Sibyl (whose mother is far less concerned than Kathleen's). They locate Ramón's impoverished family in Mexico, and Kathleen visits Ramón's grave. She and Sibyl wander aimlessly about the country, regularly use hard drugs, stay in fleabag hotels or on the beach, and Kathleen earns occasional money as a waitress. When Kathleen discovers she is pregnant with Ramón's child, she decides to return to Ramón's family, hoping they will embrace her as their own. While she is there, a hurricane strikes—it is tempting to see this as a gratuitous O'Dell survival episode, for it has little bearing on the substance of the story (except for the coincidence that the last time such a hurricane came was when Senora Sandoval was pregnant with Ramón, and now Kathleen is pregnant with his child). Sybil eventually returns for Kathleen, and they leave together again. But Sybil's drug use results in an automobile accident in which she dies and Kathleen loses her baby. She ends up in a drug rehabilitation center, where she becomes instrumental in helping another patient give up the habit. When she finally determines to return home, she discovers that her mother has sold their house and headed east following false rumors of her daughter's whereabouts. And here the story ends.

The resolution of Kathleen, Please Come Home is problematic, to say the least. Sybil's death and Kathleen's miscarriage are both too convenient. Now Kathleen never has to stand up to Sybil, nor does she have to assume the responsibility of raising a child. She is given virtually a clean slate, with the possible exception of a heavy conscience. Perhaps most disturbing is that, at the conclusion, Kathleen is still an underaged girl with no apparent home and no plans to return to school. Her mother's sale of the family home is completely inexplicable, bordering on the ludicrous. Character motivation is a problem, too—only Sybil seems to be credibly motivated on her path to self-destruction. We do not learn enough of Kathleen to be persuaded that she could so completely fall under Sybil's spell. Yes, Kathleen and her mother have their differences, but theirs seems fairly typical of mother–teenage daughter relationships. Readers seeking to comprehend Kathleen's irrational behavior must draw the conclusion that we are all vulnerable creatures, living in a delicate balance, and that, as the writer of Ecclesiastes tells us, "time and chance happeneth to them all" (9:11). This is a weighty message for teenage readers, but O'Dell undoubtedly believed the stakes were too high to treat this subject lightly.

The diary format is an unusual technique for O'Dell, and it causes some interesting problems. By its very nature, a diary typically records events of a given day, and we would expect that the fluctuating moods of the writer would be recorded as well. But these diary entries lack that sense of immediacy. Consequently, the passage describing Ramón's death, ostensibly written on the day Kathleen learned about it, appears almost clinical—quite uncharacteristic of a passionate teenager who is swept up in a whirlwind romance. A similar problem exists in Mrs. Winters's recording the events of the day Kathleen disappeared. She describes the rather mundane activity of preparing breakfast, in which she was engaged prior to discovering that her daughter had run away. Such attention to unimportant details seems uncharacteristic of a diarist's concerns on what must have been an extremely stressful day. Only an outside narrator—either omniscient or a subjective consciousness—could credibly have set the stage in this way. O'Dell wants to dramatize the events, and many are worthy of dramatization, but the diary seems not to be the best vehicle for that.

Critics have also noted that the book sends, at best, a mixed message regarding drug use. The following passage is Kathleen's description of her first experience with a hallucinogen:

> As I spoke the poem, the words glided out of my throat and hung in the air. They no longer were little squares but hovering butterflies that looked like jewels. Oh, so sweet and beautiful . . . Music came from far off. It was the music of the stars rubbing together, touching, lingering, kissing—millions of stars, and I was a star, too, the very center of all the worlds God had ever created.
>
> It was a heavenly moment that seemed to last a million, million years . . . I was richer than anyone in the world, than anyone who ever lived, than Croesus . . . Then an angel's hand plucked me from the tree and I floated earthward like a dandelion puff in a soft, soft breeze full of friendly voices and the odors of all the perfumes in the world.[6]

This is hardly a stinging indictment of the use of hallucinogenic drugs. The passage is altogether too tantalizing, the words too magical, the experience almost enticing. Critics generally praised *Kathleen, Please Come Home* for its gripping story—it does contain excitement, and we are compelled to keep reading further. One critic noted that it has "all the trappings of a made-for-television movie."[7] Another felt that "the novel is archetypical, deeply moving and profound. With this book, O'Dell has moved to a new level" (Rumbaugh, 75). The heavy dose of reality was undoubtedly influenced by O'Dell's service on the board of directors of a tranquillity house for children with drug problems, an experience that must have given him considerable insight into the tormented lives of addicted teenagers (Wintle and Fisher, 176–77). But, as with many problem novels, the book has not worn well. The problem novel, when it does not explore the psychological depths of the human condition, is rather quickly dated as teenagers drift from fad to fad in their eternal struggle to break the parental bonds and make their own distinctive mark on the world. But even if they have their flaws, both *Child of Fire* and *Kathleen, Please Come Home* demonstrate the depths of O'Dell's own passion and his empathy for the delicate balance in which the lives of so many troubled adolescents are suspended.

The Spanish Smile

In *The Spanish Smile* (1982), O'Dell again turns to contemporary life— although the bizarre circumstances recounted in the story are more suggestive of an eighteenth-century Gothic novel than a tale of present-day California. Lucinda, the narrator, is the daughter and only child of an eccentric multimillionaire, Don Enrique de Cabrillo y Benivides, a descendant of an old Spanish family who lives on an ancestral estate comprising the entire Isla del Oro (a name resurrected from *The Captive*), off the southern coast of California. Don Enrique despises the twentieth century and refuses to have electricity or any other modern innovation on his island. He keeps his daughter in the lap of luxury, financed by a fabulous gold mine on the island (which he has managed to keep a secret from the rest of the world), but he also keeps Lucinda a virtual prisoner, even forbidding her to read any work written in the twentieth century.

Initially the story focuses on Don Enrique's struggles against the encroachment of the Americans and their ways, which threaten the old

Spanish civilization he is trying to preserve. However, the novel rapidly devolves into a macabre horror story. In the first chapter, Lucinda recalls a childhood visit to her eccentric paternal grandmother on the mainland. The scene O'Dell describes is either surreal or silly, depending on how much patience the reader has. Her grandmother receives Lucinda in state, and she uses an Indian boy as a footstool (this is the third time O'Dell has used that image, but here it is ludicrous to imagine that such behavior would be tolerated in the twentieth century).

Don Enrique is convinced that his wealth can buy anything. He has decided that he wants to bring the remains of a famous Spanish explorer, Juan Rodriguez Cabrillo (a real sixteenth-century figure who died on San Miguel Island), to be buried in the crypt on the Isla del Oro. In fact, he announces that he wishes to bring the remains of *several* Spanish explorers to his island, including Pizarro and Father Junípero Serra. It is not clear why this crackpot idea does not strike Lucinda as particularly odd, but she reports it in the same tone that we might expect if she were describing her father's wish to transplant jacaranda trees in the castle courtyard. As a matter of fact, Lucinda's greater concern is that her father reneges on his promise to let her go to the mainland for her 16th birthday. It is one of the book's difficulties that Lucinda describes the erratic, crazed behavior of her father without seeming to realize that it is erratic and crazed. When she finally comes to the realization that he is mad—in chapter 14—the reader wonders why on earth it took her so long.

Chance brings a young archeologist, Christopher Dawson, to the island, who is coerced into helping Don Enrique with his exhumation project. Throughout the book Lucinda harbors a crush on Dawson and projects him into her fantasies, all based on the books she has read—he is Heathcliff to her Catherine Earnshaw, Count Vronsky to her Anna Karenina, Apollo to her Daphne. Eventually, Dawson will be instrumental in uncovering the dark secret of Don Enrique.

Early in the book, Lucinda recounts the story of her mother's disappearance. A beautiful woman who is unable to tolerate her husband's neglect, she falls in love with a painter. Outraged at his wife's alleged infidelity, Don Enrique orders a closet in his wife's apartment walled up (in the manner of Poe's "The Cask of Amontillado") where he presumes the artist is hiding. At the same time, his wife, Lucinda's mother, disappears. Lucinda tells us that it is occasionally rumored that both her mother and her lover were walled up. Despite this horrifying possibility, Lucinda has for 10 or more years lived with her father, obeyed him, and

even respected him—it is difficult to understand how she has maintained her sanity. Since his wife's disappearance, Don Enrique has
brought a series of beautiful Anglo women, usually blonds without
apparent talent or intellect, who remain on the island for a short time
and with no apparent purpose, then are ultimately sent packing—so
Lucinda is led to believe—to be replaced by another. Lucinda is astute
enough to note that these women are not her father's mistresses, and
their role remains a mystery until near the end.

At Dawson's urging, Lucinda attempts to escape from the island but
is quickly discovered and returned. Her attempt seems not to ruffle her
father, who, in fact, takes her into his confidence (quite inexplicably
unless we realize that he is mad and nothing he does makes sense) and
reveals his outrageous plan to seize the San Onofre atomic power plant
and occupy it until California is liberated by the United States and
returned to Spanish rule. Lucinda points out to Don Enrique how
absurd his plan is, but incredibly she does not yet reach the conclusion
that he is indeed mad.

The most macabre development is a discovery made by Dawson while
preparing for another burial in the crypt. Dawson takes Lucinda and
Dorothy D'Amico, the latest of Don Enrique's Anglo women, down to
the crypt where a secret passage leads to a chamber filled with crystal
coffins containing the embalmed bodies of all the other Anglo women—
women, Lucinda explains, of the "race that had humiliated Spain, a race
upon whom my father had sworn everlasting revenge."[8] The tale gets
still more absurd. Don Enrique is bitten by a poisonous snake in the
crypt and dies. The island doctor, Gerda Wolfe, who is responsible for the
embalming, is discovered to be a Nazi war criminal, and Lucinda and
Dawson manage to prevent her escape. (There is some nonsense about
her conducting secret experiments on the dead women, but O'Dell is
never very clear about that.) Lucinda's attorney—one person who turns
out to be trustworthy, which itself is surprising given Don Enrique's
shady enterprises—locates her mother in the West Indies. Lucinda, now
the mistress of the island, has the wall in her mother's apartment
removed, and the closet is discovered to be empty (which surely must be
a disappointment for O'Dell's young readers). Lucinda then sets about to
bring the modern world to her island and to generally improve the lot of
her "subjects." All in all, it is an overlong denouement, and most readers
will feel that things have worked out far too easily, given the original
state of affairs. The story does not lack for drama and intrigue, but for
the discerning reader it falls far short of O'Dell's capabilities.

The Castle in the Sea

The Castle in the Sea, the sequel to *The Spanish Smile*, was published in 1983. The story resumes several months after the bizarre events in *The Spanish Smile* have concluded. The villain is now Villaverde, the demonic and crazed servant of Don Enrique, who is determined to continue his dead master's desires. Villaverde has been named Lucinda's guardian in her father's recently discovered, but not yet probated, will. The threat of Villaverde's guardianship casts a shadow over the Isla del Oro. Lucinda, now 17, faces mounting problems on her island estate, a result of years of mismanagement and neglect under her father's regime. Questions are raised concerning illegal aliens and deplorable working conditions in the extraordinary gold mines that form the foundation of Lucinda's fortune, and, inexplicably, the bodies of the women her father killed remain embalmed in their crystal coffins in the crypt. (We might legitimately ask why the authorities have not investigated some of these matters, but the answers are not forthcoming.)

Villaverde is every bit as mad as Don Enrique, and, as with Don Enrique, no one seems to notice. He is convinced that the Isla del Oro still belongs to Spain and that American law does not apply to the island. To complicate matters further, Lucinda's fiancé, a Spanish nobleman, Don Porfirio Puertoblanco, has arrived from Spain with his mother, Dona Octavia, who is pressing for a quick marriage. This marriage had been arranged years before by the parents, and the two principals have never met. We suspect from the beginning that Villaverde is opposed to the marriage for it would end his prospects of guardianship. Don Porfirio, who is conveniently a student of metallurgy with a keen interest in the workings of the gold mines, bears scars of an attack by thugs just prior to his leaving Spain. He becomes a central character, cold and distant personally and anxious to take on the reins of responsibility for the island (he is prone to using the pronoun *we* when he refers to estate affairs, a habit of great annoyance to Lucinda).

Villaverde brings a woman from Spain, Dona Catalina de Portago, whom he wishes to be a confidante for Lucinda, but she is a thinly disguised spy for Villaverde. Two other characters complete the principal cast list: Dr. Beltrán, the new island physician (and a Muslim, which makes him immediately suspect in Villaverde's and Don Porfirio's eyes), and Father Martinez, the island priest, both of whom are clearly supporters of Lucinda, but who are not particularly effectual against the power and influence of the sinister Villaverde.

The loosely constructed plot chronicles a series of mysterious occurrences all designed to frighten or harm Lucinda. A mysterious presence is felt in the library, and a half-smoked cigar suggests that Lucinda's father has returned to haunt the castle (but the cigar disappears when Lucinda tries to show it to others). She finds a cryptic note in what appears to be her father's handwriting. And someone has been moving the crystal caskets containing the embalmed bodies of the women. (In a perplexing decision, Lucinda had agreed to sell the bodies to a showman. Mercifully, she changes her mind. The inclusion of the bodies seems only to enhance the sense of the macabre.) Lucinda seeks help from the physician, who believes her condition to be psychological, and from Father Martinez, who chastises her for not taking action and assuming her responsibilities on the estate. Through several chapters we follow Lucinda and Porfirio as they inspect the mines—and Porfirio barely escapes death in what appears to be an accident, although Lucinda rightly thinks otherwise. Lucinda then finds a deadly bushmaster snake in her bedroom, and she is now convinced that someone is trying to kill her, a fear reinforced by a second mine accident, this time involving herself.

Yet another "accident" befalls Porfirio when his horse charges through a mirror. Dr. Beltrán saves his life, but his face is disfigured. He briefly suspects the doctor of deliberately disfiguring him, but his jealousies are never long-lasting: he is far more interested in Lucinda's gold mines than in Lucinda. And finally, the climactic "accident" occurs when a huge chandelier falls on the harpsichord during the great party and kills, not Lucinda, who was scheduled to be playing, but Dona Catalina, who had to substitute for her at the last moment when Lucinda was beset by a fit of hiccups.

At long last detectives from the mainland are called in, and all fingers point to Villaverde. He finally confesses to the crimes, even to having hired the assassins to kill Porfirio while he was still in Spain. (They failed in the attempt, which explains why Porfirio arrived on the island injured.) However, Villaverde is crazed, and he has set explosives to destroy the castle. Lucinda escapes, as do Dona Octavia and Father Martinez, but we hear nothing of anyone else—except that Porfirio is presumably one of the victims (which is convenient for Lucinda, since she had already told him that she did not love and could not marry him). The castle sinks dramatically into the sea.

These brief summaries will suggest how far the two novels stretch the reader's credulity. The first-person narrative proves a handicap in both cases, forcing the victim of a nefarious plot to appear naive in her own telling (or else give away the secrets). *The Castle in the Sea* is even less tightly woven than *The Spanish Smile,* and the characters of Dr. Beltrán and Father Martinez eventually seem to serve no purpose—indeed, it is Porfirio who performs the truly heroic deeds of helping to bring Villaverde down and saving the lives of others, and he is killed in the final blast. No character is very fully developed. In addition to her naïveté, Lucinda is incapable of action and falls too readily under the influence of others. Dr. Beltrán and Father Martinez both act as confessors and show sensitivity, but they too are never allowed to carry through with significant actions. Porfirio has the potential to be a true gallant, but we are never absolutely sure whether he cares for anything but the island's gold. If there is an overriding theme to these books, it is O'Dell's favorite attack on the corrupting influence of wealth, which has the power to drive men mad.

One critic said of *The Spanish Smile* and *The Castle in the Sea* that "they are entertaining because of the mystery, intrigue, and multiplicity of far-fetched episodes, motives, and effects" (Usrey, 292). Indeed, one reviewer confesses of *The Spanish Smile* that "I couldn't put it down as I waited for the next wonderfully unbelievable thing to happen."[9] *The Castle in the Sea* received much less favorable press. One reviewer was particularly biting:

> Disappointing best describes this novel. The characters are shallow and easily confused. The story line is difficult to follow with events left vague and unexplained. O'Dell's free use of Spanish words and phrases only muddles things more. The reader is not endeared to any character and is left indifferent to the ending. Unfortunately, attention will be drawn to this novel due to O'Dell's previous award winning works.[10]

Another reviewer points out that "[p]erhaps offered tongue in cheek, the tale would have been more successful."[11] Surely, the preceding plot synopses attest to the soap opera quality of the novels, and if we accept them on that level, they can be a great deal of fun. In fact, these pieces of Gothic horror fiction might have succeeded if they had been parodies of the genre rather than rambling, confused stories that take themselves far too seriously. We suspect O'Dell himself recognized their weaknesses, for he never attempted anything similar again.

Alexandra

Alexandra, published in 1984, is a true work of contemporary realism, without the Gothic milieu and melodrama of *The Spanish Smile* and *The*

Castle in the Sea. The story is set on the Gulf Coast of Florida, where the Greek immigrant Stefan Dimitrios, a retired sponge fisherman, and his family live on Anclote Key, near Tampa. Stefan, now an old man, has a son, Elias, who is a sponge diver, a daughter-in-law, Athena, and two granddaughters, Daphne and Alexandra. It is, of course, a first-person narrative told by Alexandra, the younger granddaughter, now in her mid-teens.

The story opens on an anxious family awaiting word of Alexandra's father, who has been involved in a sponge-diving accident. We are introduced to the handsome Spyros Stavaronas, a shrimp fisherman whose family old Stefan hates because of rumors that they contributed to the deaths of Jews in World War II. This remains a suspicion, and nothing ever comes of it. Alexandra is infatuated with Spyros, losing her lead in a swim race because she catches sight of him and loses her concentration. But Spyros is too old for her and has his sights on her elder sister. When Alexandra's father is brought home suffering from the bends, he refuses proper medical treatment and dies, cryptically uttering the Greek word *alazonia,* which means arrogance. Inexplicably, we see little of the family's grief, and grandfather Stefan plans almost immediately to take out their boat, the *Cybele,* and sponge fish with Alexandra as the diver. Her mother's objections are futile.

Much of the first half of the book reads like a tract on sponge fishing, and we see Alexandra adapting easily to her father's profession. In fact, she acquires almost celebrity status as a teenage, female sponge diver. In the course of their fishing expeditions, they encounter Spyros's ship, an impressive shrimp boat, and Alexandra and her grandfather are invited aboard for an elegant dinner. Back at Anclote Key they sell their sponges to the highest bidder, a shady character named Kanarsis (he offers twice the highest offer and pays in cash). The two boat hands, Parsons and Tasso, are mysterious figures as well, and before long Alexandra notes that both men are flashing about a considerable amount of money—far in excess of what her grandfather pays them. She also learns that Daphne is now quite serious about Spyros.

All the threads eventually come together. Alexandra accidentally discovers packages of cocaine hidden in sponges that had been strung up to dry on their ship. She deduces that Parsons and Tasso are responsible and now realizes why Karnasis had been willing to pay an outrageous price for mediocre sponges. She also suspects that Spyros is involved and that the invitation to dinner on his ship had been a ruse designed to permit the transfer of cocaine.

Alexandra keeps all this a secret from her grandfather. Spyros and Alexandra's older sister, Daphne, have announced their engagement, and Alexandra is reluctant to believe the worst about Spyros. He, of course, denies complicity when she confronts him, but he is given away by Tasso who comes to him asking for money. When Alexandra discovers a bag of cocaine in Daphne's purse, she realizes she must do something. She takes the *Cybele* to Tampa to inform the Coast Guard authorities, and on the way she tells her grandfather all she has learned. And so the story closes without our learning the consequences of Alexandra's actions. For many readers, the conclusion is unsatisfying and openended. One reviewer even predicted that a sequel was forthcoming.[12]

Alexandra is a much closer knit story than *The Spanish Smile* or *The Castle in the Sea*—and much more convincing as contemporary realism. But O'Dell is, almost by nature, a didactic writer and most comfortable when describing a people's culture and mores. Because the cocaine-trafficking adventure does not allow him to explore the Greek American heritage of the Dimitrios family, he must compensate with either a gripping plot or a character study. The plot contains suspense, but at times it moves almost imperceptibly, and then suddenly rushes to its inevitable conclusion. The characters of Alexandra and her grandfather are not fully realized. They face remarkably few struggles—either physical or intellectual. Alexandra's sponge diving is so successful and so nearly effortless that it seems almost recreational (and this despite the fact that her father died as a result of his job). Further, turning in Spyros to the authorities appears to have required little soul-searching—after all, he had just spurned her for her older sister. It all seems too easy.

Alexandra received mixed reviews. Some praised its "proliferation of local color"[13] and its adventure and romance. But most agreed that the characterization of Alexandra was insufficient, that the plot superceded the character. On the other hand, the plot sometimes carried O'Dell away from the Greek American culture he wished to celebrate. The conflict between cultures that ordinarily so fascinated him proved to have little bearing on this story. Nor is the theme of greed and its devastating effects explored in any depth. The best chapter is the one that describes Alexandra's underwater confrontation with a giant loggerhead turtle, a scene reminiscent of Karana's most valiant moments. The book does contain a fine portrait of an intergenerational relationship—that between Alexandra and her grandfather. It is her grandfather, the most memorable character in the book, who utters the best line: "What you have yet to learn is that the deepest waters are not out in the Gulf but somewhere deep inside you."[14]

Black Star, Bright Dawn

O'Dell's last piece of contemporary fiction was *Black Star, Bright Dawn,* a brief work, almost a novella, published in 1988. It is the story of a young Eskimo girl's adventure in the Iditarod, the famous thousand-mile dogsled race between Anchorage and Nome, Alaska. The story is narrated by Bright Dawn, the daughter and only child of an Eskimo couple who are caught between two worlds—their native culture and the rapidly encroaching white civilization. After her father, Bartok, loses his fingers to frostbite in a near fatal seal-hunting accident, the family relocates from their isolated Eskimo fishing village to a larger town, where her father is forced to take work in a cannery. His sinking spirits are revitalized when his boss offers to sponsor him and a team of sled dogs in the Iditarod. Bright Dawn is his constant companion during the training, and when her father is injured he persuades his sponsors to accept his daughter in his stead. And so the story becomes a coming-of-age novel in which the protagonist discovers her inner resources and finds a direction for her future.

Bright Dawn endures the grueling training and with the aid of her capable lead dog, Black Star, undertakes the hazardous race. On the trail she meets Oteg, a native Eskimo who lives by the old beliefs, the beliefs that Bright Dawn and her parents have been reluctantly giving up. He shares with her stories of King Raven, a trickster figure, and she comes to admire his closeness to nature. Oteg is not competitive, however, and seems disappointed when Bright Dawn, determined to win, eventually leaves him behind. Nature strikes with a vengeance—blizzards, subzero temperatures, and treacherous ice flows all test the mettle of Bright Dawn. She persists stubbornly to the end. She does not win the race, even though at one point she is close to doing so. But she wins a $2,000 bonus for being the first to reach the village of Iditarod. A life-threatening experience on an ice floe, similar to that which nearly killed her father, removes any chance of her winning. However, she does finish, which is itself a significant achievement because nearly half of the competitors do not. And, more important of course, is that the accomplishment has taught Bright Dawn a great deal about herself. She is given the Sportsmanship Award and the $2,500 that accompanies it in recognition of her selfless aid along the way to her fellow racers.

Aside from the obvious theme of perseverance in the face of adversity—a variation on the survival story—O'Dell is pressing for a celebration of cultural integrity. Bright Dawn's parents raised her in the old traditions, and, when she enters the white school in the town of Ikuma where they move after her father's accident, she is confronted with a new culture. Religion poses one of the first problems, for in the church (a luxury not afforded their home village of Womenga) she hears confusing stories from the Reverend Cartwright, stories "about God and the Devil, about heaven and hellfire."[15] Bright Dawn explains that she had always believed in the native god named Sila:

> Sila is a mystery. He lives far apart from us, way off in nothingness. No one has ever seen him. No one has ever heard him speak. But he watches to see that we do not harm the world we live in—the air and water, our friends the animals, the land and the sky. If we do harm them he will become angry and all of us will vanish from the earth like a mist in the morning. (*Black,* 19–20)

The passage is typical of O'Dell's expressions of the wisdom of native religious creeds—faiths that hold close to nature and demand harmony among all life. Oteg, Bright Dawn's sometime companion in the race, practices the native beliefs. He performs a dance with knives to summon the more pleasant South Wind; he clings to the stories of King Raven. Bright Dawn has heard these stories in her youth and confesses, "I did not believe much in Raven and his power, though more than the Reverend Cartwright thought I did" (*Black,* 41). Gradually, Bright Dawn, forced to live close to nature, trusting only in her instincts and her team of dogs, comes to see the wisdom in many of the old ways.

The old ways imply a pact with nature—necessitated by the fact that so much of living is accomplished in nature—on the tundra, in the forests, on the sea. As in Jean Craighead George's *Julie of the Wolves,* survival often means giving up part of our humanness and surrendering to something more fundamental. At one point Bright Dawn sleeps in an abandoned cabin and encounters a mother wolf and her pups also using the shelter. But Bright Dawn and the wolf develop a mutual trust, and they even communicate: "I lay still and spoke to her in the wolf talk I used with Black Star. She answered me with the same tones. The tones rose and fell. They were wild, not even close to being human, yet as clear to me as spoken words" (*Black,* 80). This is the sort of communion with nature that Karana enjoyed as well.

The story is told with simplicity, as befits its youthful narrator, and contains some thrilling scenes. It is not a work of particular subtlety. The themes are often treated rather heavy-handedly. For example, in the final chapter Bright Dawn's mother suggests that she should go on to college, become a teacher, and return to their village to "help our children. . . . They're caught between two worlds, their own and the white world" (*Black,* 102). And Bright Dawn herself remarks after the race is over, "I was not the same person who had left Ikuma long weeks ago. How I was different, I didn't know. But it was there, deep inside of me" (*Black,* 103). The work may be too brief to effectively handle the rather complex themes, and the clash of cultures is not explored sufficiently. Bright Dawn's parents, after all, enter the white world only after her father's accident results in a bout of depression that prevents him from functioning in his native village. This seems not so much a matter of white civilization encroaching as actually offering Bartok another chance. The white owner of the cannery that employs the rehabilitated Bartok is the one who puts up money enabling first him and then Bright Dawn to race. The theme of cultural identity seems to have been superimposed on a simple adventure story—sometimes it fits, and sometimes it does not. Nevertheless, this is one of O'Dell's most successful pieces of contemporary fiction—it is fast-paced with characters we care about and scenes we will remember. It is also closest in spirit to his best historical fiction, steeped as it is in local culture, grounded in a serious theme, and focused on a humble, but noble, character who has something at stake.

Conclusion

Writing about contemporary American life did not come easily to O'Dell. The romantic in him sought the out-of-the-ordinary, the culture on the fringe, and the charm and fascination of the past. The wide variety of fictional forms O'Dell experimented with after his string of successful historical novels in the 1960s and early 1970s suggests that he wanted to keep his writing fresh. Even though contemporary fiction proved not to be his strong suit, his insistence upon returning to it in various forms—problem novel, Gothic romance, modern adventure story—is a sign of his vitality as a writer. Even into his eighties, he was not afraid of departing from established and comfortable patterns and venturing into what was for him the unknown. That he did not always succeed matters little in the final analysis. We can justly admire a writer who refuses to stagnate and sink into complacency, but who approaches each new project with daring and a sense of adventure. It was a spirit that kept Scott O'Dell vibrant for over 90 years.

Chapter Eight
A Return to Many Pasts

Love is a bridge but it's not made of stones. It's made of the dew on the rose, the flaming bush, the shy smiles of children, birds in the meadow, a fall of snow on a winter day.
—O'Dell, *The Road to Damietta* (1985)

It is, of course, as a historical novelist that Scott O'Dell will be chiefly remembered. The historical novel, it seems safe to say, was in his blood, the blood that once coursed through the veins of his venerable ancestor and the father of the historical novel, Sir Walter Scott. In his last decade, O'Dell explored a variety of historical times and places—medieval Europe, sixteenth-century Jamestown, the Caribbean of the eighteenth century, the American Revolution, the Pacific Northwest at the beginning of the nineteenth century. He also found himself attracted to well-known historical figures—Saint Francis, Pocahontas, Sacagewea—as well as to the less famous. The historical fiction of the 1980s is reminiscent of vintage O'Dell, steeped in the history and geography of the place, attacking greed and injustice wherever they occur, and celebrating the irrepressible human spirit.

Sarah Bishop

In the late 1970s, O'Dell moved to Westchester County, New York, to a house located near a cave that had acquired local fame as the onetime home of an eccentric woman of the late eighteenth century. O'Dell became intrigued by the woman, who was named Sarah Bishop. The real Sarah Bishop had appeared mysteriously in northern Westchester County sometime toward the end of the eighteenth century. She always carried a musket with her and lived in a cave much of her life, occasionally rooming with local inhabitants for whom she would perform odd jobs. She died in 1809 during a fierce snowstorm and is buried in North Salem, New York. When O'Dell heard her story, he wondered what would cause a woman to abandon society so thoroughly. This became the kernel for *Sarah Bishop,* published in 1980. In *Sarah Bishop* O'Dell departs from both of his favorite story venues: the Southwest and the sea. He would prove, however, adept at depicting the eastern seaboard, and in succeeding novels he would explore a rich variety of settings. O'Dell's interests in Sarah Bishop's story are many. The way in which the Revolutionary War divided families—Sarah's father was a staunch royalist, her brother a rebel (or patriot, depending upon one's point of view)—is dramatically illustrated. Sarah wrestles with her urge for revenge (both her father and brother are casualties of war) and her desire for inner peace. She is also torn between the individual's conflicting needs for society and for solitude. The harmony of the natural world and humanity's need to embrace that harmony are prominent forces reminiscent of *Island of the Blue Dolphins*. O'Dell draws on familiar themes and uses his strengths to advantage.

The first few chapters demonstrate the divisive nature of the American Revolution, as Sarah is caught between her father, an outspoken and deeply religious loyalist, and her brother Chad, a youthful, idealistic champion of the rebel cause. The family is treated poorly by the local miller and his rebel cohorts, and O'Dell draws some very fine character portraits showing us some of the more unsavory views of the revolutionaries. O'Dell's refusal to romanticize the war follows in the tradition of Christopher and James Lincoln Collier's *My Brother Sam Is Dead* (1974), another story of divided family loyalties during the American Revolution. Chad and his friend David Whitlock, who reads to the family from Thomas Paine's *Common Sense,* announce that they are enlisting. Old Mr. Bishop is devastated and their parting is chilly. Sarah and her father are tormented by the rebels, their horses stolen, their buildings burned, and, finally, Mr. Bishop is tarred and feathered. He dies as a result of the injuries, leaving Sarah with nothing in the world, save for a fierce determination.

Sarah takes a job in the kitchen of a nearby inn to discover information about her brother, who, she learns, is a prisoner in New York. She heads there and in an exciting turn of events is mistakenly accused of setting fire to Trinity Church in a desperate attempt to free her brother. She is held by the British and eventually persuades an officer to take her to the prison ship to see Chad, but she arrives too late, for he had died earlier that morning. Sarah escapes from the prison and flees back to the inn, but it is unsafe there. She turns to Mrs. Jessop, one of her father's few friends, but Sarah cannot tolerate the old widow's prattling about religion. Sarah has become embittered and skeptical. She leaves Mrs. Jessop's, taking her father's Bible, and in the woods she reads the passage from Matthew 5, verse 44: "Love your enemies, bless them that curse you, do good to them that hate you . . ."[1] But Sarah's suffering has been so overwhelming, her grief so complete, that her response is to rip the page from the Bible and burn it.

Sarah flees north to the wilderness, working along the way for food, shelter, and a little money, with which she purchases a musket from a ferryman. A man named Goshen, who gives her a ride, attempts to sexually assault her, but Sarah escapes with her horse. Goshen will continue to be her nemesis in her efforts to flee society. She eventually reaches a deserted cave and transforms it into a home. At this point, the novel takes on the appearance of a survival story. O'Dell describes the steps Sarah must take to prepare her home for winter. She befriends a white bat, a playful creature whom she names Gabriel, after the archangel. She is visited by an Indian named John Longknife and his wife, Helen, who is part English. With their help she begins to hollow out a log for a canoe. These instructional survival chapters, reminiscent of *Island of the Blue Dolphins,* are an O'Dell trademark by now.

Sarah settles in for the winter, during which she must contend with the insufferable Goshen. While in town for supplies, she meets a young Quaker named Morton who befriends her. Numerous adventures prove Sarah's mettle, but her antisocial behavior causes her to be accused of witchcraft by the neighboring townspeople. Young Morton pleads on her behalf, but to no avail. All seems lost until, in the nick of time, a postal rider arrives from Boston and reports that the drought and sickness are spread throughout the entire region from Boston to New York and not isolated in their community. His testimony persuades everyone that Sarah is not the cause of their woes and she is absolved. Readers are likely to find Sarah's last-minute rescue through the chance arrival and testimony of a postal rider contrived, to say the least, although most will also feel that it is about time she had luck on her side.

Morton cannot persuade Sarah to leave her cave, but he is successful in helping her to see the importance of forgiveness. When she returns to the cave and sees a copperhead snake, rather than kill it as a feared enemy, she decides to let it live. It is impossible not to be reminded of Karana coming to terms with her enemies. The book's conclusion is bittersweet, for Sarah is not reconciled with the world of men and women. She still returns to her cave, although we do see some sign of her softening: "Dusk came as I reached the western ridge. I looked back. Above the trees, down in the valley, I watched the lamps in Ridgeford village go on. It was a pretty sight, to see them light up one by one. I had forgotten how pretty friendly lights could be" (*Sarah,* 230). In these final lines we glimpse the hope that Sarah might someday resume her life with the community; however, this was not the case with the real Sarah Bishop. It is an example of O'Dell's adapting his material to suit his audience.

Sarah Bishop was received well by the critics, who acclaimed it as an exciting story with a strongly drawn central character. Its themes are several—the tragedy of war, the folly of superstition, the evil of greed, the discord between the desire for revenge and the need for reconciliation, the human need for atonement with the natural world, and, in the words of one commentator, the conflict "between the individual's need for solitude and the need for society."[2] O'Dell avoids sentimentality and even-handedly presents American Revolutionary War history. Both the British and the patriots are depicted as violent, foolish, and excessive in their zeal. Sarah is wronged by both sides. The pious Quakers are depicted as slave holders (it is a source of contention between young Morton and his father that the latter owns two slaves, whom he ultimately frees at the insistence of his son). They are also dangerously superstitious. The world is a violent place—nature, in the form of bitter weather or poisonous serpents, can be deadly; human society, in the form of ignorance and unbridled passion, can be equally deadly. Survival requires personal strength, cunning, patience, and, as Sarah eventually learns, forgiveness.

The story has also been seen as a study of grief. Sarah, who has lost everything and everyone that meant anything to her, strikes out at the world in anger. She then withdraws from humanity into her cave where she finds some peace. But her final assuagement must come with her gradual reintegration into human society, for without that society, she cannot become whole. This is the story of Sarah's rebirth. When Karana is taken from her island, we read that event as an ending. But when Sarah consents to join young Morton at another Quaker meeting and when she, in the book's last paragraph, looks with tender longing on the distant village, we sense that these events are a beginning.

The Road to Damietta

Following Sarah Bishop, O'Dell turned to completing his Seven Serpents Trilogy, publishing The Feathered Serpent in 1981 and The Amethyst Ring in 1983, and tried his hand at contemporary fiction with The Spanish Smile in 1982, its sequel, Castle in the Sea in 1983, and Alexandra in 1984. He returned to historical fiction in 1985 with The Road to Dami-

etta, a story of Saint Francis of Assisi, a work that, for some at least, was reminiscent of his former powers. One reviewer proclaimed, "[O'Dell] has written what may be his finest novel, [which] is unsurpassed at recreating the human beings in the orbit of St. Francis and the places where the great events of his life occurred."[3] O'Dell had long been fascinated by Saint Francis. Perhaps he was drawn to the holy man's love of the natural world and his rejection of the worldliness that had corrupted the institution of the church.

The story is narrated by Ricca Montanera, the daughter of a powerful, noble family of Assisi, who is hopelessly in love with the handsome, vivacious, and outrageous Francis Bernardone, son of a wealthy cloth merchant. Ricca, a typical headstrong and independent-thinking girl of 13 when the story opens, adores Francis's free spirit and his youthful rebellion, but he takes little notice of her.

Ricca earns her father's displeasure by allowing Francis to free a costly falcon. (Francis, of course, is concerned for the imprisoned animal; Ricca is hoping to win favor with Francis.) Her punishment is confinement in her family's scriptorium, where she is "condemned" to copying the Scriptures and other works. In O'Dell's zeal "to show that women and men do have the same potential" (quoted in Commire, 118) he may be stretching history, for it is improbable that such a fate ever befell a medieval woman. A short time afterward, the youthful Francis, in penance for stealing from his father, returns his possessions to his father, including his clothes, which he returns in a dramatic gesture by disrobing in the public square. To everyone's horror, Ricca, in a trancelike state, also disrobes, imagining herself as Eve to Francis's Adam in the unashamed nakedness of their original innocence. Her act disgraces her family and has no effect on Francis, who shortly afterward commits himself to a religious life of poverty and chastity.

Ricca, undeterred, continues to pursue Francis in the hope that he will come to his senses, abandon his spiritual pursuits, and settle down with her. Her tenacity is surpassed only by that of Francis (this is really the story of Ricca's awakening and coming to terms with her love for a man whose heart belongs only to God). Francis begs for food in the streets and goes door to door seeking stones with which to build a church. At first Ricca is repulsed by the transformation, but she soon falls under his spell again—as do most people. She is jealous and suspicious when her friend, the beautiful Clare di Scifi, whom she believes is her rival for Francis's affections, tells her that Francis has asked her to organize an order of women. Ricca helps Clare escape from her family to join Francis, although she later betrays her to her family. Clare becomes, of course, Saint Clare, founder of the Poor Clares. Ricca is as incapable of understanding Clare as she is of understanding Francis—spiritual and altruistic motives are alien to Ricca. But then, average people do not, as a rule, understand saints.

O'Dell introduces an incredible bit of intrigue when Ricca learns that the bishop is writing to the pope charging Francis with heresy. At a party in the bishop's palace, Ricca manages to get into his study, find the letter, rewrite it exonerating Francis, and reseal it. Ricca's letter is sent to Rome, and Francis's troubles with the church hierarchy are put to rest. Ricca also composes a letter after the fashion of Héloïse to Abelard, but does not send it. Héloïse, surely one of the feminists of the Middle Ages, is a particular hero of Ricca's. Ricca herself makes a contribution to the cause of womanhood when, during her work as a copyist, she amends the works of Saint Augustine where he is disparaging toward women—another example of O'Dell's giving his thirteenth-century characters twentieth-century sentiments.

Eventually, Ricca's family, exasperated by her escapades, sends her to her aunt's convent in Venice, where she becomes a celebrated copyist. As luck would have it, Francis turns up in Venice, where he is preparing to join the Fifth Crusade to Jerusalem, which will take them by way of Damietta in Egypt. When she finds Francis in San Marco Cathedral and tells him her plans to go on the crusade, he suspects (correctly) that it is for the wrong reason. But the headstrong Ricca manages to reach Damietta (albeit it on a brothel ship). In Damietta, the crusade takes on the flavor of a reunion. It seems that all of Assisi has gathered—she encounters the former bishop, now the Cardinal Legate; Raul, her onetime tutor (who proposed to her once); and the neighborhood baker and his wife. Ricca becomes involved in diplomatic intrigues when she makes it known that she speaks Arabic (she is another of O'Dell's cast of accomplished linguists).

She accompanies Francis as an interpreter for the sultan. In an episode not worthy of the book, Ricca agrees, at the sultan's request, to perform the dance of the seven veils to tempt Francis, whom she still believes she can win. Of course, she only embarrasses herself—Francis proves unflappable, and she and the sultan are persuaded that he is indeed a holy man. Regrettably, the peace agreement negotiated by Francis and the sultan is ignored by the Cardinal Legate, and the city of Damietta is sacked. The angry Sultan mercilessly routs the Christians. The crusade is a complete disaster.

Ricca sees Francis only once again before his death, but she is now reconciled to the fact that her love for Francis must be unrequited. Her experiences have brought her self-knowledge. In a conversation with Clare after his death, she acknowledges: "I say that sometime he will be a saint, though this is the least of all that he would wish for himself. And that you will be a saint also—Saint Clare of Assisi. And that never, never, in this life or afterward, will I become a saint."[4]

One reviewer complained of *The Road to Damietta* that "it is often difficult to see where fact ends and fiction begins."[5] If O'Dell intended an exciting story of intrigue, adventure, and unrequited love, then he fairly well succeeds. However, readers hoping to learn about the life of Saint Francis are likely to be dissatisfied, for the details are sparse and the character elusive and underdeveloped. For much of the book, he remains an almost untouchable creature viewed by Ricca from afar. O'Dell covers a great deal of ground—chronologically, geographically, and psychologically—and he attempts to tie the narrative together with the thread of Ricca's almost obsessive-compulsive, one-sided love affair with Francis, who never once gives her the least encouragement. In time some readers may begin to lose patience and to wonder at Ricca's obtuseness. One writer correctly observes that Ricca "seems to be a young girl with twentieth-century feelings and attitudes put down in the Middle Ages" (Usrey, 293). Her chasing after the saintly Francis for nearly 20 years gives her an unseemliness and her "determination to win [him] away from his vows seems a rather ignoble goal" (Usrey, 293). This, indeed, may be the book's greatest flaw. Still, despite these shortcomings and its occasional melodrama, the book provides excitement, and the seriousness of its major themes prevails—the distinction between sacred and profane love, the importance of individual integrity, and the power of commitment. *The Road to Damietta* is the closest thing to a religious statement that O'Dell would ever make.

The 290

In *The 290,* published in 1986, O'Dell returned to a subject he had explored in his Civil War story for adults, *The Sea Is Red.* The 290 was a Confederate warship built in a Liverpool, England, shipyard under highly secret circumstances. Not even those who built her knew that she was to be commissioned in the Confederate Navy and christened the *Alabama* (290 simply refers to the ship's identification number used during construction). Although many British openly favored the South,

Great Britain was officially neutral and obliged to refrain from aiding and abetting either side in the conflict. The *Alabama* became one of the most famous and successful of the Southern raiders, sinking 69 enemy ships without the loss of a single enemy life. And although O'Dell begins with this remarkable story, he characteristically individualizes it, focusing on an American youth, Jim Lynne, a shipyard worker who opts to sail with the ship when she embarks on her missions for the Confederacy. The story quickly evolves into the adventures of Jim Lynne, and the *Alabama* fades into the background for much of the book.

Jim, the narrator, is the 16-year-old son of a New Orleans slave trader. Having left home while he was quite young to escape his father's imperious ways, Jim is unaware that his father is now one of the wealthiest slave traders in the South. He discovers this information from his brother, from whom he had been long separated and who implores him to join the Northern cause. Jim declines, still feeling an attachment to his Southern roots; however, he does deplore slavery. In this way, O'Dell can present a sympathetic Southern protagonist who is also against slavery. Perhaps Jim's sentiments reflect the influence of the British, who had outlawed slavery several decades before, but who remained largely pro-Southern (the margin was five to one in favor of the South in the House of Commons). Of course, many British still harbored resentments left over from earlier Anglo-American conflicts. But O'Dell fails to point out that the British looked upon the deplorable working conditions in America's Northern factories with the same moral disdain as they regarded Southern slavery.

At any rate, when the time comes for the *290* to set sail, Jim eagerly joins the capable Captain Semmes, a historical figure, and becomes a Confederate seaman. Captain Semmes frees Lem Wilson, a black slave serving in the galley, and Jim and Lem become fast friends. No explanation is offered for Semmes's humanitarian act, except that it elevates the reader's opinion of the captain of the *290* and demonstrates that the Southern cause was not entirely about slavery. Semmes's humanity is demonstrated further by his careful treatment of the captives taken from the Northern ships when they are seized.

Jim proves himself a hero in helping to squelch an attempted mutiny, and his reputation rises. He becomes part of a small crew charged with taking a captured ship to Haiti, where he secretly hopes to see his father's slaving establishment. Several chapters are then devoted to Jim's clever efforts to rescue slaves from his father's company and reestablish them on a deserted Caribbean island, where they can build a new life for themselves. Jim spirits away some 200 would-be slaves, provides them with tools, and thus spares them a life of bondage. O'Dell depicts some exciting scenes—midnight meetings, voodoo ceremonies, dangerous deceptions—but the entire episode may strike some readers as far-fetched.

After this prolonged episode (it occupies about one-third of the book), Jim rejoins the 290, which is on its way to France for refitting. In Cherbourg, the 290 encounters the *Kearsarge,* a Union warship, and a dramatic sea battle ensues. After a valiant fight, the 290 is sunk, bringing to a close a distinguished career, much of which Jim missed while he was freeing slaves in Haiti. Jim returns to Liverpool and resumes his old job in the shipyard, along with his friend, Lem Wilson. But shortly afterward, Jim learns that his father has died and left him everything (apparently his father was unaware of Jim's escapades in Haiti), and Jim and Lem head for America—to an uncertain future.

The 290 was not especially well received by the critics, who found it rambling, disjointed, and too much of a historical documentary to make a satisfactory novel; one critic complained that "[t]he painstaking research becomes a straightjacket."[6] Indeed, it was felt that the book would serve well as an informative supplement to history courses, which surely was not O'Dell's intention. The lengthy digression relating the events in Haiti seems to belong to another novel, and sending Jim back to the *Alabama* in time to experience its dramatic end is a plot twist that is hard to swallow. But we have seen in many of the later books that unity of narrative is a quality that often eludes O'Dell.

In many respects the book is mistitled. Much of the story does not concern the 290, and Civil War buffs hoping for an informative novel on the ship's career will be disappointed. Readers hoping for a Confederate point of view will likely be disappointed as well, for O'Dell, in his condemnation of slavery, fails to make clear the legitimacy of the Confederate cause. This is the story of Jim Lynne and his coming-of-age. As war is wont to do, it has accelerated Jim's own character growth—although for Jim, at 16, to have engineered the control of an ocean-going vessel and effected the freeing and reestablishment of some 200 slaves is an astonishing achievement, to say the least. It does not seem that his prior experiences (building ships in a Liverpool yard and a brief stint on a Confederate raider) would have prepared him for such adventures.

O'Dell is very good at capturing the spirit of an era, however. If the book's plot lacks credibility at times, it is nevertheless action-filled and contains some fine, suspenseful scenes. And as is typical of O'Dell's historical fiction, the reader will come away with a clear sense of the author's moral stance and purpose. O'Dell wishes to depict the sensitivity and depth of humanity as experienced by a Southern seaman—history is too often told from the victors' point of view. O'Dell's fundamental humanitarianism, his abhorrence of oppression of any kind, and his faith in the individual (as opposed to society) all emerge strongly from the pages of *The 290*. For O'Dell, history is never simple, and that always comes through in his novels, even if, at times, he does not completely succeed in unraveling history's complexities.

Streams to the River, River to the Sea: A Novel of Sacagewea

O'Dell returned to the western American tales he loved in *Streams to the River, River to the Sea: A Novel of Sacagewea*, published in 1986, the same year as *The 290*. Telling the story of Sacagewea was probably inevitable for Scott O'Dell, given his great interest in both female protagonists and Native Americans. Sacagewea, of course, is one of the most famous Native American women, celebrated as the guide for the quintessential American explorers Meriwether Lewis and William Clark.

Streams to the River, River to the Sea covers chiefly that part of Sacagewea's life dealing with her experiences with Lewis and Clark, although the book opens with an attack on Sacagewea's Shoshone village by the Minnetarees. Sacagewea and her cousin, Running Deer, are taken captive, but virtually everyone else, including Sacagewea's mother, is murdered. Sacagewea is assigned to the chief's household and is intended as a wife to the chief's eldest son, Red Hawk. Before the wedding can take place, Sacagewea is stolen away to a rival village, ruled over by a brute called LeBorgne. She escapes under cover of night and survives on her own in the wilderness. She befriends a buffalo cow, only to see it shot and killed by a trader named Toussaint Charbonneau, who is part French and part Indian. He returns her to the Minnetaree village, where she is claimed simultaneously by Charbonneau, Red Hawk, and LeBorgne, who decide to have a contest to determine who will have her. Charbonneau wins, they are wed, and soon Sacagewea is pregnant.

Shortly before her baby arrives, Lewis and Clark come to the village seeking a guide. Accompanying them is Ben York, a black slave, who intrigues the villagers, who have never seen a black man before. Lewis and Clark want to employ Charbonneau as their guide, and it is understood that Sacagewea, whom Clark insists on calling "Janey," will accompany them. He also helps her with English and teaches her to write. On the journey, Sacagewea digs roots for the men to eat and, in fact, plays a relatively minor role in the expedition. But this is a fairly accurate representation of Sacagewea's contribution, for it was her husband, Charbonneau, who was the guide. Charbonneau, however, proves unreliable and, at times, untrustworthy. Sacagewea even wonders if he is an agent of the Canadians trying to sabotage the expedition.

A boat accident deprives them of most of their food and nearly results in the loss of Clark's journal, which Sacagewea rescues. They must resort to killing a mother grizzly, to Sacagewea's dismay ("It is bad luck to kill a bear that has a young one at her side"[7]). Sacagewea, like Karana, has a particular affinity for animals, and she is horrified when she sees some Blackfoot Indians lure a herd of buffalo over a cliff to their deaths. (We must suspect that these sentiments are more the product of O'Dell's twentieth-century sensibilities than those of the historical Sacagewea in the nineteenth century.) The focus of much of this part of the book is on finding food and simply surviving—a favorite theme of O'Dell's. Charbonneau proves to be ill tempered, and Clark must intervene at one point when Charbonneau strikes his wife for not having a fire ready. As for Sacagewea, she discovers that she is falling in love with Clark.

After grueling hardships, the expedition finally reaches the Pacific, where a fort is built; then they must make the return trip, which requires much less narrative. Charbonneau has proven a thorough scoundrel, having taken another wife, who bears him a baby girl. Clark offers to take Sacagewea to the East with him to educate her and her son, Meeko, in the white ways. Sacagewea, however, must choose her native ways, and leaves the village to return to her own people and land, without saying goodbye to Clark, for she knows it would be too painful. Thus her story ends with a bittersweetness that may very well have characterized the life of the real Sacagewea.

O'Dell has taken the framework for this novel from the *Journals of Lewis and Clark.* Indeed, very little is actually known of Sacagewea. Even in the *Journals,* she is usually referred to as "Charbono's [sic] Indian woman." One of the more detailed incidents is recorded by Lewis, who notes that Sacagewea's labor was "tedious and the pain violent" until she was given a portion of the rattle of a rattlesnake. Within 10 minutes her son was born.[8] It must have been tempting for O'Dell to make Sacagewea into a more heroic figure than he did, but he chose to restrain that impulse, perhaps to remain reasonably faithful to what historical facts were known. However, the larger reason must surely have been that since it is Sacagewea herself who is telling the story, she must not be made to appear boastful. The result is a character of stoic beauty, undertaking a treacherous and exciting journey with a newborn baby strapped to her back.

The use of the first-person narrator presents some interesting problems in the book. At one point, for example, Sacagewea tells us, "Every day Captain Clark made black marks in a thing called a journal. He made marks with a stick he dipped in black paint. He said the marks were words that told everything he had seen or heard or thought that day" (*Streams*, 66). The naïveté of these words belies the fact that Sacagewea must, at the time she tells this story, already have known about writing instruments and paper. But, as always, O'Dell opts for the immediacy of the first-person narrative, assuming its risks as well.

The continuity of the book—its dramatic action—is sometimes broken by a lack of direction. The book has an almost episodic structure, with little interconnectedness between episodes—threats of starvation, canoe accidents, Indian attacks, and encounters with wildlife. And there is the inescapable fact that once the explorers reach their goal—the great Pacific—they must turn around and go back home. That it takes 24 chapters to get Sacagewea to the sea and just 3 to get her back to her people suggests that O'Dell himself recognized the limited possibilities of the narrative.

O'Dell's Sacagewea lacks the heroic qualities of the Sacagewea of myth. But O'Dell has given us a flesh-and-blood heroine who endures real physical and spiritual hardships. If she seems to be reduced to a food gatherer who is compelled to take this marvelous journey not out of a love for adventure or a quest for knowledge but because of her infatuation with a man, that is simply O'Dell's way of giving her a believable existence. Also, we must remember that she is telling her own story and she is, by nature, a self-effacing individual.

Streams to the River, River to the Sea contains the familiar O'Dell themes. A conflict of cultures is evident throughout, and, as is also typical of O'Dell, the conflict is not simply between the Native American and white cultures. The Native American cultures are often at odds among themselves, although Sacagewea's peaceful Shoshone people clearly have O'Dell's admiration. But along with the conflict of cultures, we also see O'Dell's conviction that peoples of different backgrounds can successfully live and work together.

This book received more favorable reviews than most of O'Dell's later historical fiction. He seems more self-assured when writing of the American West and Native American cultures and when he is expressing his conviction about those cultures' affinity with the natural world. This conviction is revealed in the concluding paragraphs of the novel, paragraphs that, in their stark simplicity, are particularly moving:

> In the morning we were on the trail at sunrise. The sky was deep blue and cloudless. Locusts sang in the high grass. The wild blooms of summer were everywhere. I picked a handful for Meeko.
> He laughed and smelled them. One day when he was older I would tell him that the wild blooms were the footprints of little children, those who had gone away and had come back to gladden us. I would tell him many things that the Shoshone people knew. (*Streams,* 163)

The Serpent Never Sleeps:
A Novel of Jamestown and Pocahontas

Fresh from his novel about one Native American heroine, O'Dell launched immediately into a story that would feature another. *The Serpent Never Sleeps,* which appeared incredibly in O'Dell's 90th year, 1987, is billed in its subtitle as *A Novel of Jamestown and Pocahontas.* The true protagonist and narrator is a young English girl named Serena Lynn, who, when the story opens, is an attendant to the formidable Countess of Foxcroft, a slave trader who is heavily invested in the Jamestown settlement. As luck would have it, Serena encounters King James I hunting near the countess's castle, and in a short time Serena and the king are on quite familiar terms. One of the more astonishing scenes describes James's gory ritual after the kill, in which he steps inside the bloody carcass of the slain deer, recites the witches' lines from Shakespeare's *Macbeth,* and smears the blood over his own body. The king appears to draw strength from this peculiar act. He gives her as a parting gift a ring in the shape of a serpent.

The king returns a few weeks later to attend the countess's masque, which is being given to raise money for the failing colony of Jamestown. Among the guests at the masque are William Shakespeare and his children, Judith and Hamnet. (O'Dell's history is uncharacteristically faulty here, since Shakespeare's son Hamnet died in 1596, 13 years before the countess's masque. The error is more egregious because the inclusion of

Shakespeare is so superfluous to the story.) At the masque, Serena's love, the countess's impetuous son Anthony Foxcroft, kills one of the retainers in the royal retinue and must flee. Serena's passion causes her to give up an opportunity to become the queen's secretary and to follow Foxcroft to Plymouth, where together they sail to America, but Foxcroft is discovered and imprisoned aboard the ship.

The sea voyage is long and hard, and a hurricane blows them off course to Bermuda, which proves to be a veritable paradise. There factions arise: some wish to remain in Bermuda, others desire to press on to Jamestown. In any event, a new ship must be built. Foxcroft dies in a brave attempt to sail to Jamestown in a small boat to let the settlers know the rest are on their way. (Foxcroft's untimely death is a convenience, for it eliminates a troublesome character who would necessarily have to be tried—and probably put to death—for his transgression in England. Now he is allowed to die a hero, and Serena can get on with her life.)

At long last, the new ships are ready, and the colonists sail to Jamestown only to find most of the inhabitants dead or dying—there are even reports of cannibalism. The greatest problem is the settlers' fear of the Indians. Serena, who has heard the moving stories of Pocahontas and John Smith, believes that she must find the princess and implore her to intervene with her father on the colonists' behalf. With remarkably little effort, Serena finds Pocahontas and establishes a cordial relationship with her—although softening her father, Powhatan, is not so simple. So the settlers must limp along, braced by the arrival of five new ships from England sailing under the leadership of De La Ware. In the meantime, Serena is courted by Tom Barlow, but she still carries a torch for the dead Foxcroft.

A second expedition is sent in search of Pocahontas, and Serena accompanies it. (Like most of O'Dell's protagonists, Serena enjoys linguistic fluency, having acquired a knowledge of the Algonquin tongue.) The English kidnap Pocahontas, and during her captivity she and Serena become fast friends. Pocahontas even shares her secret name with Serena, a sign of utmost trust. The capture of Pocahontas does not have the desired effect, for an Indian attack ensues and Tom Barlow is seriously wounded. Serena, with the help of Pocahontas, nurses him back to health, an act cementing their relationship, but there is little passion involved. Pocahontas herself is wooed by John Rolfe, whom she eventually marries, and that marriage brings about a peace treaty between the settlers and the Indians. The story concludes with Serena's description of the remainder of Pocahontas's short life—the birth of her son, her voyage to England to meet the king, and her death there. This is a story that cries for passion, but has none. Serena is more mature than most O'Dell protagonists, and we might expect her to be a romantic heroine. But the love affair between Serena and Anthony Foxcroft has no depth and seems only a mechanism to bring about Serena's journey to the New World. Further, her relationship with Tom Barlow seems based on pragmatism and not passion. Barlow is a decent man, but, more important, he is available, and he and Serena must acknowledge their mutual need for each other if they are to survive in the harsh wilderness of the New World.

The book's title derives from the ring given Serena by King James and the symbolism surrounding it. Of the ring, the king tells her,

> You will see . . . that the ring you wear takes the form of a serpent. The serpent's coiled thrice round in a circle, thus depicting the soul from birth to ascension. You will also see that the jeweled eyes are half-closed. Do not be deceived. Neither night nor day, in all of life's strange maneuvers, do the eyes ever sleep. Beneath their hooded lids they silently observe, and upon what they observe, should it threaten your life, they quickly act.[9]

The king, however, warns her that the ring cannot protect her from harm arising from jealousy or greed. And it turns out that jealousy and greed pose the greatest threats to Serena—the jealousy of leaders of the Jamestown colony, always at odds with each other, and the greed of the English entrepreneurs who finance the New World settlements. At the same time that he gave her the ring, the king touched Serena's forehead with his bloody finger and left a mark. Although no one else seems to notice it, the mark mysteriously remains visible to Serena, another talisman intended to protect her. But by the conclusion of the story, Serena herself has begun to wonder if the ring and the mark are talismans protecting her or memories of the past haunting her.

Serena is not especially religious—in fact, some of her views on this subject are disturbingly modern and make her less convincing as a seventeenth-century Englishwoman. When John Rolfe agonizes over his love for Pocahontas because she is a heathen, Serena exclaims to herself,

> What effrontery! What arrogance! For the first time I saw clearly the gulf that separated us from the Indians. How could there ever be peace between us while white men looked upon the red men as barbarians, a group to exploit and to murder, if necessary? (*Serpent,* 163)

Of course, these are O'Dell's long-held sentiments, but we might rightly question whether a young, unschooled woman of King James's England would harbor such thoughts. When Tom Barlow's cabin is set on fire during an Indian attack at the end of the book, Serena tosses the serpent ring into the fire. It had been for her a crutch, and she no longer has need of such a talisman. She realizes that her own strength of character will serve instead. When she discards the ring, the mysterious bloody mark on her forehead also disappears—a sign that she is now her own woman. As symbols, the ring and mark are not especially powerful (the mark is more puzzling than anything else, seeming to ascribe to a foolish and superstitious king more credit than is due). Had the symbolism been elaborated on and had we seen more clearly its impact on Serena, it might have been more effective.

The story is filled with historical tidbits about life and politics in seventeenth-century England. O'Dell manages to include a description of the Gunpowder Plot, engineered by Guy Fawkes to blow up Parliament and King James I. We learn of the translation of the Bible commissioned by the king (and taken largely from the work of William Tyndale—the subject of O'Dell's *The Hawk That Dare Not Hunt by Day*). The sojourn on Bermuda is even taken from historical records. As almost always with the historical novels, O'Dell enriches his narrative with a plethora of historical information.

My Name Is Not Angelica

My Name Is Not Angelica, the story of an eighteenth-century slave revolt in the Danish West Indies, was published in 1989, making it one of O'Dell's last books. The revolt occurred in 1753, and O'Dell recognized the potential drama in the situation. The narrator is a young girl whose African name is Raisha, and her story opens in Africa, where her people are taken into slavery by a ruthless native king, Agaja, who has made his kingdom rich by enslaving other Africans and supplying them to the Europeans for the New World slave trade. In the process of this enslavement, Raisha is separated from her family, whom she never sees again, and is packed onto a slave vessel, where she and several hundred others suffer under deplorable conditions, and many die from the plague. Their inhumane treatment is unspeakable. For example, one African boy is lowered into the water on a rope so that he might plug some of the leaks in the ship with oiled cloth. Raisha reports, "One moment he was there, dangling with the rope around his waist, the next moment only half of him was there. Sharks had gotten him."[10] Raisha, her betrothed, Konje (who would have been the chief of their people in Africa), and Dondo, another friend, are sold as a lot to a Danish family, the van Proks, of Saint John Island. Raisha becomes the personal servant of Jenna van Prok, who names her Angelica for her docile and obedient nature. Life at the van Prok estate is made unbearable, ironically, by the black overseer, called the bomba, who hates the slaves. In short time, Konje, a natural leader, hatches a plot to escape. He is soon joined by runaway slaves from all over the island, and they gather at a hideout near the coast to plan their revolt. The ominous mood of the story is punctuated by the incessant beating of drums from Konje's camp, drums that transmit messages to the other slaves. The Danish governor, Gardelin, and a Lutheran minister, Isaak Gronnewald, arrive from Saint Thomas, bringing supplies to quell the rebellion. Governor Gardelin's method is characteristically draconian, invoking even more severe laws punishing runaways. Gardelin and van Prok are symbols of European oppression and arrogance. Jenna van Prok, however, grows increasingly distraught over the deepening crisis and turns to drink. Isaak Gronnewald makes feeble attempts to thwart a confrontation, and he seems to be a sincere man, but he can offer little hope to the slaves and no advice aside from imploring them not to flee. (The minister recalls a host of well-meaning but ineffectual clerics that populate O'Dell's novels, tokens of his skepticism that institutionalized religion could solve social problems.)

With each chapter the feverish pitch grows. For Raisha, the crisis comes when Dondo attempts to rescue a slave boy from a brutal beating. Dondo himself then suffers a horrifying death on the rack at the governor's orders, Gronnewald's intercession having failed. With this, Raisha flees into the night, but she cannot join Konje's camp because they have no food. So Raisha survives on her own, after the manner of Karana and Sarah Bishop, for nearly a month. At last, Raisha heads for the runaway camp with a supply of fish she has caught. Shortly afterward, Gronnewald arrives at the camp to warn the runaways that the governor's men are on their way. Gronnewald, honoring their betrothal, consents to marry Raisha and Konje.

The denouement comes quickly after this. With the aid of French troops, the governor raids the runaways' camp, and Gronnewald is killed by French soldiers as he is trying to negotiate. In the face of massed soldiers, the runaway slaves leap from a cliff to their deaths rather than return to bondage. Although Konje leaps to his death, Raisha, who is pregnant with Konje's child, will not sacrifice the child's life. An afterword tells us that Raisha was taken to the French island of Martinique, where she worked for a French sea captain for a year. Then, according to French law, she and her baby daughter were freed.

O'Dell is very good at creating mood. The beating drums, the oppressive heat, and the nagging insects all help to establish the ominous atmosphere in which inhumane acts are perpetrated. This atmosphere reinforces O'Dell's principal themes—the desperation of an oppressed people and the insensitivity of the oppressors, who are corrupted by power and greed. But O'Dell does not retreat into using stereotypes, and the van Proks and Reverend Gronnewald are all individuals, each of whom deals with the issue of slavery quite differently. Likewise, O'Dell portrays a variety in the characters of the Africans—it is an African king who originally sells Raisha's people into slavery, and it is an African who so brutally oversees the van Proks' slaves. It is this balance in his reportage that gives O'Dell's historical fiction its veracity and power. The book's title suggests Raisha's insistence on maintaining her cultural identity and rejecting the European name thrust upon her by Jenna van Prok. In reality, however, Raisha clings to little of her native culture, and the enslavement seems to have effectively destroyed the cultural distinctions of the Africans. (The most notable sign of this is that Raisha and Konje are married by a Lutheran minister.)

Finally, Raisha's will to survive in the face of the voluntary deaths of her husband and every one of her friends may not be persuasive, but it does provide a hopeful ending (and enables her to narrate the story). Raisha's survival, which rather handily results in her freedom, makes the mass suicide seem ill begotten. Why could not all of the runaways have been taken to French territory and eventually freed? This is the all too convenient conclusion to which O'Dell often succumbed. One wonders, if he had been able to abandon the first-person narrator and perhaps dared to write the death of his protagonist, whether the story might not have been more powerful and more convincing—if less suitable for a young audience. On the other hand, O'Dell generally preferred not to leave his created worlds submerged in despair. He insisted on letting hope peer above the horizon, finding, even in the darkest moments, a glimmering of humankind's redemptive spirit.

Thunder Rolling in the Mountains

Scott O'Dell's last book was still an uncompleted manuscript when he died in 1989, and his wife, Elizabeth Hall, herself a writer as well as her husband's confidante, was able to complete the book in accordance with his wishes. *Thunder Rolling in the Mountains* is a story of Chief Joseph of the Nez Percé, and as Chief Joseph's story is one of the darkest in the annals of the American West, so this is one of O'Dell's darkest books. Narrated by Sound of Running Feet, Chief Joseph's 14-year-old daughter, the book tells of the forced migration of the Nez Percé, of their subsequent conflict with both the whites and other Native American tribes, and of dissension among their own ranks.

In the first chapter, Sound of Running Feet happens upon white settlers encamped illegally on land belonging to the Nez Percé, or as they call themselves, Ne-mee-poo. The encounter underscores the animosity between the two peoples. The whites ironically accuse the Ne-mee-poo of having too much land and being greedy. The whites also insist on calling the Ne-mee-poo the "Nez Percé," French for pierced nose, even though piercing noses was not their custom. But, the narrator points out, "when the whites decided something was so, nothing could change their minds."[11]

Upon the deaf ears of the American General Howard, Chief Joseph pours out his feeling of passionate attachment to the land, an attachment that comes from genuine love and not from a greedy desire to possess and exploit it. The chief's attitude, of course, is incomprehensible to Howard, who, like most whites in the story, sees land as wealth and power. The gentle Chief Joseph is no match for the ruthless American military, and when he is ordered to remove his people from the land, he acquiesces, believing that the alternative would be massive bloodshed. However, Chief Joseph's decision causes a rift among the tribe as many of the younger warriors prefer to stay and fight, including Swan Necklace, who is betrothed to Sound of Running Feet. Chief Joseph prevails, but Swan Necklace and an unruly warrior named Wah-lit-its kill two white men, making war a certainty.

The Indians win an important battle against the whites, but they continue their journey, hoping to find a peaceful place to settle. A subsequent assault by the whites leaves 31 Nez Percé dead and 26 wounded. Running Feet's own mother dies. Chief Joseph laments, "All men were made by the same Great Spirit Chief. Yet we shoot one another down like animals" (*Thunder,* 57). The devastation is bewildering as more of the wounded die. Running Feet's infant sister is nursed by a woman who has lost her child. An old woman, suffering from serious wounds, asks to be left behind to die. Her request is honored. For their own survival, the Nez Percé must take to raiding, stealing horses, and even killing settlers (but humanely not scalping them, it is pointed out). When they take two white women captive, Chief Joseph proclaims, "[W]e do not kill women" (*Thunder,* 72). Running Deer is amazed that "the white women acted no different from women of the Ne-mee-poo" (*Thunder,* 73). This is one of the principal lessons of all of O'Dell's multicultural fiction: to seek our inner commonality despite our outward differences.

Another unsettling reality is revealed when the Nez Percé find that the Crow Indians are actually fighting with the whites against them. Worn out by hunger, betrayed by the Crow, the Nez Percé are finally defeated and taken prisoners, but Running Feet and Swan Necklace escape, hoping to find Sitting Bull and implore him to help. They are taken in by Assiniboin Indians, where they are once more betrayed— Swan Necklace's throat is slit. Running Deer is forced into a marriage with a brutish Assiniboin, Charging Hawk, but manages to escape during the marriage celebration. Charging Hawk pursues her, but she eludes him and, significantly, passes up her chance to kill him. She has seen enough bloodshed in her short life and now walks alone to "the Old Lady's Country" (that is, Canada), where she hopes to find peace. The afterword tells us that Sound of Running Feet reached Sitting Bull's camp and remained there a year before marrying a Ne-mee-poo named George Moses. Her father, Chief Joseph, died a broken man in the state of Washington, never seeing his daughter again.

Perhaps no O'Dell story is so unremitting in its pessimism, its parade of violence and death. The glimmer of hope to which readers have become accustomed in O'Dell's work is indeed faint, perhaps acknowledging the historical record of the defeat of the Native Americans, the virtual destruction of their civilization, and the triumph of a people who had proven themselves to be crass, insensitive, greedy, and malicious. However, the betrayal by the Crow and Assiniboin suggests that O'Dell's concern is not a culturally specific one; good and evil exist in all peoples. His despair, instead, is over the power inherent in humanity to destroy itself through hatred, intolerance, avarice, and fear. *Thunder Rolling in the Mountains*—the title is taken from one of the names of Chief Joseph—is a sobering work, and because of that it puts O'Dell's primary concerns in their proper light. He always flirted with the dark side of humanity; it is fitting that his final work should be one of his most audacious flirtations.

Chapter Nine
Critical Assessment

Whether remembered or imagined, all of my stories are in a certain sense written not for children but for myself, out of a personal need. Yet all of them exist in the emotional area that both children and adults share.

—O'Dell, quoted in *Something about the Author* (1990)

Scott O'Dell's achievements are considerable. A great many of his books are still in print and undoubtedly will remain so for a long time to come. When we consider the body of his work, several elements emerge as worthy of notice: he was a good storyteller, a master of historical fiction, a champion of multiculturalism, a lover of the natural world, and a defender of moral integrity.

The Storyteller

O'Dell's greatest strength was that he was a fine storyteller. He knew how to pace a story, how to build suspense, how to establish atmosphere. Nevertheless, in his stories, we can readily detect a formulaic quality, and the formula can be described thus:

- A youth is thrust by chance into a situation calling for extraordinary perseverance.
- The youth is typically alone but occasionally may find a trustworthy, although largely ineffectual, companion.
- The youth takes the high moral ground and is pitted against usually older antagonists who are driven by greed for power and worldly wealth.
- The youth displays impressive leadership qualities, sometimes acquired under the tutelage of the antagonist.
- Through cleverness, resourcefulness, and luck, the youth proves to be a survivor—often the only reward is survival. Few of the protagonists find wealth, but they do achieve security and self-actualization.

Thus we have O'Dell's formula for the *bildungsroman,* which is really what most of his fiction is. The youthful protagonist comes to maturity through great hardship, and the reception into the adult world is not always a happy one. It is interesting to note how many of O'Dell's protagonists ultimately settle upon a solitary, or near solitary, life—Estéban de Sandoval (*The King's Fifth*), Bright Morning (*Sing Down the Moon*), Carlota, Sarah Bishop, Julián Escobar (The Seven Serpents Trilogy), Raisha (*My Name Is Not Angelica*), Sound of Running Feet (*Thunder Rolling in the Mountains*), and others. But we should not take this as O'Dell's rejection of society. O'Dell typically sets his stories in civilizations in crisis, many under threat of invasion or on the verge of collapse. O'Dell always takes the side of the oppressed, and if his protagonist belongs to the dominant civilization—Estéban or Sarah Bishop, for example—we find the protagonist rejecting that civilization. But for many of his protagonists, embracing the society that nurtured them is not an option. His heroes and heroines are left with little choice than to head out on their own, armed with their own strength, resilience, and determination. And so his works speak of the triumph of the individual in the face of both physical and spiritual adversity.

Scott O'Dell is not an eminently quotable writer. His prose is generally simple and straightforward, seldom elegant, seldom even memorable. At times, O'Dell could write a sentence such as this conundrum from *The Hawk That Dare Not Hunt by Day:* "Then, as planned, I met Phillips in the Alcazar, not that day, but next, less than a week from the afternoon two months before when we had parted at Cadiz."[1] But generally, O'Dell's writing is direct and to the point, without a great deal of physical description, and seldom reflective. If it is rarely music to our ears, neither is it pretentious or unapproachable. And on occasion he achieves the near lyrical, as in this passage from *The Road to Damietta:* "Love is a bridge but it's not made of stones. It's made of the dew on the rose, the flaming bush, the shy smiles of children, birds in the meadow, a fall of snow on a winter day" (*Road,* 217).

O'Dell began his career as a novelist writing in the voice of the omniscient narrator. In both *Woman of Spain* and *Hill of the Hawk* he makes judicious use of the third-person narrator, revealing the story from multiple points of view. In both these works, which are about the clash of cultures in old California, O'Dell is able to provide a more balanced perspective than he could have achieved with a first-person narrator. However, in his last novel for adults, *The Sea Is Red,* he turned to the first-person narrator. And, curiously enough, it is precisely this choice of narrator that makes this work less than satisfying, for the narrator of this adventure story is required to be phenomenally ubiquitous as well as multitalented, and as a result he emerges as rather immodest. O'Dell, nevertheless, seems to have felt more comfortable with this point of view, for he used it in every succeeding novel, save for the two novellas he wrote for early elementary school-age readers.

Undoubtedly, he was encouraged by his successful use of the first-person narrator in *Island of the Blue Dolphins*, where Karana's voice adds immediacy and quickly summons our sympathy. In that book, however, part of our willing suspension of disbelief is not to ask questions about the circumstances of the narration. When and to whom was Karana supposed to have delivered this tale? The sequel, *Zia*, makes it perfectly clear that she was unable to convey the slightest information about her sojourn to her rescuers; she did not speak their language and she died soon after. Lois Kuznets praises O'Dell's use of the first-person narrator in *Island of the Blue Dolphins* for its helping

> the young reader to overcome a distance from a protagonist of another race and time. The use of a central consciousness might not at the same time have enabled O'Dell to leave the epilogue—where it would not overshadow the affirmation of the novel—the ironic, historically accurate ending to Karana's struggle to create a community on an island abandoned by humans.[2]

At the same time, Kuznets acknowledges the limitations of the first-person narrator, seeing, along with Henry James, that it "may be used to prevent 'real contrast' with the consciousness of the central character, who can be an unreliable witness even of his or her psychological events" (Kuznets, 189). This lack of reliability is particularly important to consider with children's writers, who are typically portraying child characters. Frequently, the most sensible, if not necessarily the easiest, method for the children's author is to use an omniscient narrator or a central consciousness and thus avoid problems of linguistic style and even psychological understanding. Kuznets writes,

> In practice and in contrast to the first-person point of view, the use of a central consciousness seems frequently to give freedom to the author to expand the boundaries of language aesthetically. An author may use syntactically complex and imagistic prose that might seem realistically inappropriate to a child or even adolescent narrator, and, hence, produce a stylistically dense work. (Kuznets, 190)

One of the best-known and most successful uses of a central consciousness in children's literature is found in Laura Ingalls Wilder's "Little House" books, where the reader sees the world through the wide-eyed innocence of Laura (who is only five in the first book of the series) but enjoys the language of a somewhat more sophisticated literary stylist. O'Dell chose this option only twice—for *Journey to Jericho* and *The Treasure of Topo-El-Bampo*—in the former, perhaps, because his hero is very young, and in the latter because his heroes are burros.

The King's Fifth is perhaps the best example of O'Dell's use of the first-person narrator. In this story, the narrator has both a logical reason and the wherewithal for telling his tale. He is passing time in jail by recording his memoirs. Perhaps O'Dell was thinking of another Spaniard, Cervantes. But never again would O'Dell trouble himself with justifications, and his readers are asked to accept as credible narrators people who often seem to have no cause for sharing their tale, let alone a rationally explainable means of doing it. Sacagewea's telling her own version of the Lewis and Clark expedition seems bizarre at times—particularly when she confesses not to understand the concept of writing. Perhaps this is an oral retelling? The preceding may seem like nitpicking, but the choice of narrator is not an arbitrary matter. The first-person narrator demands a credible means and justifiable reason for imparting his or her knowledge to the reader—something we do not always get from O'Dell. Of his use of the first-person narrator, O'Dell acknowledges that he was influenced by the work of Joseph Conrad. But he also remarked, "I think it's the easiest way to write . . . because you don't have to work so hard for suspension of disbelief. When you read that 'I did it' there's a tendency to believe what you're being told. You get an almost automatic identification which I think is so important in a story" (Wintle and Fisher, 176).

The Historical Novelist

The historical novel, a noted critic tells us, "is distinguished among novels by the presence of a specific link to history: not merely a real building or a real event but a real person among fictitious ones. When life is seen in the context of history, we have a novel; when the novel's characters live in the same world with historical persons, we have a historical novel."[3] At the same time, most historical novels do not take historical personages as their protagonists; rather they use more typical individuals whose lives are shaped by the historical events and people surrounding them. In this respect, the historical novel is often the story of social change. Consequently, the historical novelist must possess a coherent worldview—a dominant social vision—or else the result will be a meaningless hodgepodge of dubious historical data and myth. O'Dell's achievement as a historical novelist is that he does have such a worldview. We will examine some of the details of that view in the balance of this chapter, but first we should consider how O'Dell handles some of the problems facing the historical novelist.

One of the most pressing difficulties of the writer of historical fiction is how to impart historical data without unnecessarily overburdening the narrative. Historical fiction has much in common with utopian fiction and science fiction in that all these literary forms require the writer to divulge a certain body of information about the politics, sociology, technology, and religion of the society in question. But the historical facts must remain unobtrusive; the action must remain paramount. O'Dell is very good at keeping the plot his focus, generally not allowing the minutiae of daily living to overcome his narrative—as is so easy to do in historical fiction. And, because so many of his historical novels involve peoples from two distinct cultures coming together, O'Dell's narrators have the perfect excuse for exposition. (Hence, Julián Escobar, a Spaniard, relates with relish the details of the Maya, the Inca, and the Aztec civilizations.) Also, we never feel that O'Dell is giving us a history lesson. His interest remains in his protagonist as a human being, not as a pawn of history. The historical figures always play minor roles—seldom more than walk-on parts. O'Dell is generally careful not to make his novels quasi-historical reports.

One temptation to which historical novelists are particularly vulnerable is that of imbuing characters with traits not authentic to the period in which they live. O'Dell occasionally succumbs to this, most frequently when he endows his female protagonists with a greater spirit of independence than we would likely find in a woman of an earlier era. The medieval Ricca in *The Road to Damietta* and the seventeenth-century Serena in *The Serpent Never Sleeps* are two notable examples. Most often, O'Dell's female protagonists are forced to assume more aggressive stances because of the need to survive in a hostile environment—Karana and Carlota come to mind. O'Dell's treatment of character in his historical fiction is grounded in a simple philosophy—that is, "the fundamental human is about the same as he was a couple of thousand years ago. The basic changes have not been vast. Human needs for love, affection, understanding, a chance to succeed at something, are about the same" (quoted in Wintle and Fisher, 172). Sometimes a fine line exists between basic human traits and specific cultural influences. Because O'Dell typically has a strong moral purpose in his novels, his protagonists—regardless of the time or place they inhabit—tend to exhibit some decidedly twentieth-century values: a belief in individual human dignity, an abhorrence of oppressive and totalitarian regimes, a skepticism about religious institutions, a tolerance of foreign cultures. If O'Dell had to choose between maintaining historical authenticity and promulgating his own moral convictions, the latter always won out.

The Moralist

O'Dell himself was unabashed about the didactic messages in his novels:

> I want to teach and say something to people. Adults have pretty well established their lives, but you can say something to children. If you can get their attention and their affection, then there is something that can really be done with children. You can tell a story and add something that might be of interest and importance in their lives. (Wintle and Fisher, 173)

By the same token, to suggest that O'Dell was a moralist is not meant to raise specters of eighteenth-century religious fanatics scribbling dogmatic religious tracts for the edification of the young. On the contrary, Scott O'Dell was not a particularly religious man. In fact, he seems to have had an aversion to established religion. Few of his protagonists profess any profound religious affiliation. Saint Francis of Assisi must be excepted, of course (and admittedly he is not the true protagonist of *The Road to Damietta*). But even in that case we find the saint at odds with much of the religious establishment, which is probably what drew O'Dell to Saint Francis in the first place. Invariably, O'Dell associates the church with oppression and depicts its priests as narrow-minded, worldly, and lacking compassion. When the priests are not portrayed in an outright negative light, they are depicted as helpless or ineffectual. Father Francisco in *The King's Fifth* properly admonishes Estéban against the evils of greed, but he remains essentially passive as Mendoza obliterates the native population. On the other hand, O'Dell never suggests that religion itself cannot be a positive force; it is humankind that has perverted it.

For O'Dell, the greatest evils in humanity include greed for both
wealth and power and insensitivity to the needs of others. O'Dell was
particularly distressed about the emphasis modern society placed on
money: "The country is poisoned by money, so that anybody who
doesn't get rich and make a lot is considered a failure. There's none of
the old idea, still around in some places of the world, that you do your
work because you enjoy doing it" (Wintle and Fisher, 177). O'Dell
attacks avarice at every opportunity. Karana's people are defeated
because of greed (their own and that of the Aleuts), Estéban de Sandoval is nearly defeated because he allowed greed to cloud his judgment, *The Black Pearl* and *The Dark Canoe* both focus on humanity's
obsession with wealth, and throughout the Seven Serpents Trilogy
greed for gold and desire for power are the driving forces of destruction.
In his later novels, O'Dell, while still occasionally attacking humanity's
avaricious nature, began to dwell on the need for mutual understanding
between peoples. Virtually all of the novels of the 1980s address the
need for disparate cultures to lay aside their differences and recognize
their fundamental common ground. His protagonists—Sarah Bishop,
Pocahontas, Sacagewea, Raisha, Sound of Running Feet—are all caught
in the conflict between two cultures, the more powerful bent on
destroying the weaker. Never was O'Dell's social conscience so transparent. As has been suggested earlier, O'Dell seems to have been at heart
always a young people's writer, imbued with the high-minded ideals we
often expect of those writing for our youth. "I am didactic; I do want to
teach through books," O'Dell professed. "Not heavy handedly but to
provide a moral backdrop for readers to make their own decisions. After
all, I come from a long line of teachers and circuit riders going back two
hundred years" (Commire, 118).

This is not to suggest that all children's writers are didactic or moral-
istic, or that they ought to be, but traditionally most do adhere to a
fairly clear vision of an ethical world where wrong is punished and right
triumphs. The children's writer tends to present a world of possibilities,
of hopes, of dreams, and only rarely does the children's book dish up the
bitter herbs of unremitting sorrow or devastating violence. O'Dell could
write of the bleak side of life, and he could express hopelessness—*Child
of Fire* and *Kathleen, Please Come Home* are the most notable examples.
But he is not at his best in that mode. We almost get the feeling that he
did not want to believe those stories himself. His own view of humanity
was much more positive.

The Environmentalist

Scott O'Dell was ahead of his time as an advocate for the environment. *Island of the Blue Dolphins* was inspired by his outrage at the meaningless slaughter of seals. One of his favorite themes is that of the individual's survival in a harsh and unpredictable world. And invariably the key to survival is the recognition that humanity must live in concert with nature; once this is achieved, all is well. O'Dell himself recognized his debt to Daniel Defoe—and his departure from him:

> Once, in Defoe's day, we were cunning manipulative children, living in a palace of nature. In her brief lifetime, Karana made the change from that world, where everything lived only to be exploited, to a new and more meaningful world. She learned first that we each must be an island secure unto ourselves. Then, that we must "transgress our limits," in reverence for all life.[4]

O'Dell's environmentalism, in his books at least, never goes much beyond his belief that all creatures are sacred and that humankind is not superior to the rest of the animal world. Although he never wrote of pollution or the loss of rain forests or the dangers of nuclear power or land mines, we can be fairly well assured that his sentiments were against the arrogance of human progress at the expense of a simpler, more harmonious world. When we consider O'Dell's attitude toward nature, we might recall Whitman's remarks in "Song of Myself":

I think I could turn and live with animals, they are so placid and self-
    contain'd,
I stand and look at them long and long.
They do not sweat and whine about their condition,
They do not lie awake in the dark and weep for their sins,
They do not make me sick discussing their duty to God,
Not one is dissatisfied, not one is demented with the mania of owning
    things,
Not one kneels to another, nor to his kind that lived thousands of
    years ago,
Not one is respectable or unhappy over the whole earth.

Whenever O'Dell wants to show the evil side of human nature, he merely has to depict a needless slaughter of innocent animals—a mother grizzly bear slain with her cub at her side or a herd of buffalo driven over a precipice, such as he relates in *Streams to the River, River to the Sea*. For O'Dell, the natural world may, at times, be harsh, but it is indifferent. The sun shines and rain falls equally upon the good and the bad. Malevolence is the province of the human mind alone.

The Multiculturalist

Twenty-two of O'Dell's 26 novels for children have as their central characters individuals from cultures other than European American; the overwhelming majority are from Native American and Hispanic (in the broadest sense of the term) cultures. O'Dell was among the first children's authors to portray Native American characters with sympathy for their mistreatment at the hands of the Europeans and European Americans and with respect for their cultural beliefs and mores. In *Zia, The King's Fifth, Sing Down the Moon*, and *Thunder Rolling in the Mountains*, O'Dell's sympathy clearly lies with the native peoples and against the imperialist white society that overpowers them. An underlying poignancy runs through much of O'Dell's work precisely because he does lament the loss of the native societies that knew so well how to live in harmony with nature. O'Dell presents an almost idyllic view of these societies. In the closing paragraph of *Zia* the narrator describes the home to which she returns in Edenic terms:

> There was a wide stream that came out of the mountains and flowed slowly back and forth between oak trees and sycamores and the red manzanita. It had a sandy bottom with patches of blue stones. The stream was near to my home. When I came to it I began to run. My dog ran at my side. (*Zia,* 179)

Even at the close of *Sing Down the Moon,* when Bright Morning, her husband, and young son are exiled from their homeland and living in a cave, she can still draw strength from the beauty of the world around her, the world of nature that is an integral part of her existence:

> I had not gone far when out of the tall grass I saw a ewe looking at me. She turned away as I reached her, but did not flee. Her coat was thick and full of burrs. Beside her was a lamb, not more than a few days old. . . .

My son touched the lamb once before the two moved away from us. He looked up at me and laughed and I laughed with him. Rain had begun to fall. It made a hissing sound in the tall grass as we started toward the cave high up in the western cliff. Tall Boy had finished the steps and handholds and now stood under the cave's stone lip, waving at us. I waved back at him and hurried across the meadow. I raised my face to the falling rain. It was Navaho rain. (*Sing,* 133–34)

It is this affinity with nature that O'Dell cherishes about the Native American, but he is no sentimentalist. O'Dell even confessed about *Sing Down the Moon* that "I think of it as a modest tribute not only to this Indian girl but also to the courage of the human spirit. The fact that this spirit happened to be in an Indian girl is really incidental. I'm not interested in the Navajos particularly—they're not my favorite tribe even" (Commire, 117). If this seems a surprising statement from an author who spent much of his time writing about Native Americans, we should remember that only someone who had specific knowledge of various tribes could credibly make such a statement and that O'Dell's first interest was always in the human element, that which was universal, and not in the tribal.

Scott O'Dell has come under fire, however, for his characterizations of Native Americans, Hispanics, and Spaniards. He has been taken to task for his portrayal of the pre-Columbian peoples in the Seven Serpents Trilogy. In those books Mayas are depicted as bloodthirsty savages who delight in tearing out the hearts of their captives to appease their equally bloodthirsty gods. Of course, this form of human sacrifice was, in fact, practiced by the Mayas; the distortion in the picture results, as Isabel Schon points out, because O'Dell does not balance this view with the more positive aspects of the culture—the Mayan "achievements in engineering, agriculture, writing, astronomy, calendar writing, or the arts"— or the fact that "the Mayas were basically a peace-loving people."[5] Schon lambastes O'Dell's historical reporting in the trilogy rather soundly:

The trilogy is indeed a fast moving story of violence and intrigue; it is regrettable, however, that many of its young readers will be exposed to pre-Columbian cultures and the amazing conquest of Mexico through the half-truths and exaggerations of a dilettante historian. (Schon, 323)

But O'Dell's skewed vision is not directed exclusively at native peoples. He portrays the Spaniards with almost as much disdain. Today it is the popular point of view to see the Spaniards as greedy, violent fortune hunters with a misguided religious zeal and overactive libidos. But any perspective so one-sided is to be mistrusted. O'Dell frequently draws unfavorable Spanish characters. *The King's Fifth* is populated with a host of greedy conquistadores and portrays a corrupt Spanish legal system. *The Spanish Smile* and its sequel, *The Castle in the Sea,* each depict a madman of Spanish descent obsessed with returning the island he owns to Spanish rule. The Spanish people in these two novels are little more than caricatures: cold, insensitive women and pompous, strutting nobles—all drawn not from modern Spain (even though the setting is modern) but from a past that existed only in lore. Despite the fact that Lucinda, the heroine, possesses fine qualities, these works paint a very unattractive picture of Spanish culture.

However, one should not overlook the fact that in most of O'Dell's more serious works he creates a number of admirable Spanish heroes. In *The King's Fifth,* Estéban, a Spaniard of humble origins, emerges as the noblest of characters, along with Zia, a Native American girl. In *Carlota,* we find the title character, the daughter of a Spanish family of old California, to be a woman of profound integrity and great courage. (O'Dell seemed to have an easier time creating great heroines than great heroes.)

Despite his emphasis on a variety of foreign cultures (foreign, that is, to his own Anglo-American heritage), O'Dell's true interest is not so much in the culture as in the individual. In that respect, all of his protagonists have certain common features regardless of their heritage or social background. They are frequently at odds with their culture. Even Karana, who begins her life alone adhering to the values instilled by her cultural heritage, eventually becomes a rebel (if one can become a rebel when isolated on a desert island). To survive she goes against the tribal dictum forbidding women to make weapons, cavorts with her people's enemy when the Aleut girl comes to the island, and, finally, abandons some of her people's oldest social customs when she refuses to kill animals for food and clothing. In book after book, O'Dell's protagonists find themselves in positions that force them to question their cultural values, and, ironically, the result brings them closer to what most of us would call a humanitarian spirit. That spirit includes a fundamental reverence for all life, a belief in the saving grace of compassionate living. Often the protagonist must reject the norms of the establishment, which is typically portrayed as cold, insensitive, and grasping. O'Dell is at his best when he can hold his hero or, more often, his heroine up before us as if to say this is what we can become. In the face of adversity, we ultimately have only our values, our integrity. If we sacrifice them, life is not worth living. His finest heroes and heroines—Karana, Estéban de Sandoval, Ramón Salazar, Sarah Bishop—all share strong personal convictions that are put to the test in a harsh, uncompromising world. His characters seldom end up with vast riches or happy marriages—he writes no fairy tales—but they do preserve their integrity and their self-respect. And when all is said and done, the reader never doubts that that is enough.

Perhaps the most scathing indictment of O'Dell's treatment of other cultures comes from a review of *Black Star, Bright Dawn:* "There are writers able to put themselves into the mind and heart of another culture, or even sex, and make it believable. They are few, and Scott O'Dell is not one of them. He never has been. His characters are not living people."[6] This comment seems to arise not from a careful critical assessment of O'Dell's writing but from the conviction that only a member of a culture can credibly write about that culture—a view not universally held nor one that is easy to defend. In opposition to this view, Ellen Sallé reports that O'Dell received "multiple letters from children on the Navajo reservation asking what branch of the Navajo tribe he belonged to, 'since only a Navajo could have written the Newbery Honor Book, *Sing Down the Moon?*' "[7] As for *Black Star, Bright Dawn,* O'Dell received fan mail from Native Americans thanking him for articulating their struggle, not to mention a phone call from Inuit children living above the Arctic Circle who invited him to accompany them to Siberia so they could see the land of their ancestors. Obviously, O'Dell had struck a cord for those members of the cultural group about whom he was writing. Finally, Ellen Sallé writes about the success she had using *My Name Is Not Angelica* with African American children, who could clearly identify with the young African American girl taken from Africa, sold into slavery in the West Indies, brutalized, but never broken in spirit (Sallé, 26–27).

One of the most striking features of Scott O'Dell's work is his ability to assume the consciousness of almost any type of character he chose—protagonists of other cultures and races, and protagonists of both genders. In fact, in the overwhelming majority of O'Dell's novels, a female is both protagonist and narrator. The most celebrated is, of course, Karana, but there are many others—Native American Bright Morning in *Sing Down the Moon,* African Raisha in *My Name Is Not Angelica,* Eskimo Bright Dawn in *Black Star, Bright Dawn,* to name a few. This was a conscious effort on O'Dell's part, and it can be seen in his very earliest fiction. He said, "I am trying to show that women and men *do* have the same potential" (Roop, 752). Nor was he a convert to the cause of women's equality. He was always there, from his first published novel in which the central character is a strong-willed woman who holds her own against the U.S. Army and the Roman Catholic Church.

O'Dell's winning of the Hans Christian Andersen Medal seems fitting because of his universality, his genuine respect for all humanity, and his tremendous capacity for empathy. This capacity bears out the belief expressed by the great African American critic Henry Louis Gates Jr., who wrote, "No human culture is so inaccessible to someone who makes the effort to understand, to learn, to inhabit another world."[8] That, at least, should be our hope.

A Final Word

Scott O'Dell was a storyteller who realized that in his art he could advocate his own worldview. He never hesitated to attack the evil he saw in humanity. But he never forgot to praise the good. He could lament the loss of old values, but he really wished to celebrate the individual willing to sacrifice everything for those values. He was never a cynic, and, in fact, had much of the romantic in him, including a love of the natural world and the unspoken harmonies of the universe, a respect for the traditions of the past, and an admiration for the person who bravely chooses the path of integrity and honor.

O'Dell received virtually every great honor that can be bestowed upon a children's writer. This despite, or perhaps because, having once professed,

> Books of mine which are classified officially as books written for children were not written for children. Instead, and in a very real sense, they were written for myself. There is about them, however, one distinction which I feel is important to the form of literature: they were written consistently in the emotional area that children share with adults.[9]

It is this respect for his youthful audience that has earned him accolades and will account for his lasting fame.

Notes and References

Chapter One

1. Quoted in "Scott O'Dell, Interviewed by Justin Wintle," in *The Pied Piper: Interviews with the Influential Creators of Children's Literature,* by Justin Wintle and Emma Fisher (New York: Paddington Press, 1974), 180; hereafter cited in text.

2. Scott O'Dell, "Books Remembered," *The Calendar* 34 (Fall/Winter 1975–1976).

3. Scott O'Dell, "Scott O'Dell," in *Speaking for Ourselves: Autobiographical Sketches by Notable Authors of Books for Young Adults,* ed. Donald R. Gallo (Urbana, Ill.: National Council of Teachers of English, 1990), 154.

4. Quoted in "Scott O'Dell," in *Something about the Author,* vol. 60, ed. Anne Commire (Detroit: Gale, 1977), 113; hereafter cited in text as Commire.

5. Conrad Wesselhoeft, "*Blue Dolphins'* Author Tells Why He Writes for Children," *New York Times,* 15 April 1984.

6. Scott O'Dell, "Dignity of the Human Spirit," in *Children's Authors Speak,* ed. Jeanine L. Laughlin and Sherry Laughlin (Englewood, Colo.: Libraries Unlimited, 1993), 183; hereafter cited in text as "Dignity."

7. Elizabeth Hall, letter to author, 21 July 1996.

8. Errol Trzebinski, *The Lives of Beryl Markham* (New York: Norton, 1993), 240.

9. Elizabeth Hall, letter to author, 21 July 1996.

10. Austin Olney, telephone interview with author, 3 December 1997.

11. O'Dell and Hall were not, in fact, married until January 1989.

12. Quoted in Lee Bennett Hopkins, "Lee Bennett Hopkins Interviews Scott O'Dell," in *Star Walk,* ed. P. David Pearson et al. (Needham, Mass.: Silver Burdett and Ginn, 1989), 135; hereafter cited in text.

13. Scott O'Dell, "History and Fiction," *Five Owls* 3 (January/February 1990): 34; hereafter cited in text as "History."

14. Malcolm Usrey, "Scott O'Dell," in *Dictionary of Literary Biography,* vol. 52, *American Writers for Children since 1960: Fiction,* ed. Glenn E. Estes (Detroit: Gale, 1986), 295; hereafter cited in text.

15. Sally Anne M. Thompson, "Scott O'Dell—Weaver of Stories," *Catholic Library World* 49, no. 8 (1978): 342.

16. Austin Olney and Marcia Legru, telephone interview with author, 3 December 1997.

Chapter Two

1. Frederick Palmer, preface to *Representative Photoplays Analyzed,* by Scott O'Dell (Hollywood, Calif.: Palmer Institute, 1924).
2. Scott O'Dell, *Woman of Spain: A Story of Old California* (Boston: Houghton Mifflin, 1934), 299; hereafter cited in text as *Woman.*
3. Scott O'Dell, *Hill of the Hawk* (Indianapolis: Bobbs-Merrill, 1947), 148.
4. Scott O'Dell, foreword to *Man Alone,* by William Doyle with Scott O'Dell (Indianapolis: Bobbs-Merrill, 1953); hereafter cited in text as *Man.*
5. Scott O'Dell, *The Sea is Red* (New York: Holt, 1958), 281; hereafter cited in text as *Sea.*

Chapter Three

1. Quoted in Peter Roop, "Profile: Scott O'Dell," *Language Arts* 61 (November 1984): 751; hereafter cited in text.
2. Scott O'Dell, *Island of the Blue Dolphins* (Boston: Houghton Mifflin, 1960), 49; hereafter cited in text as *Island.*
3. Jon Stott, "Narrative Technique and Meaning in *Island of the Blue Dolphins,*" *Elementary English* 52 (April 1975): 442–43; hereafter cited in text.
4. R. M. Ballantyne, *The Coral Island* (1858; reprint, New York: Penguin, 1990), 338–39.
5. Ian Watt, "Robinson Crusoe as Myth," *Eighteenth-Century English Literature: Modern Essays in Criticism,* ed. James L. Clifford (New York: Oxford University Press, 1959), 163.
6. Stuart Hannabuss, "Islands as Metaphors," *Universities Quarterly* 38 (Winter 1983–1984): 78; hereafter cited in text.
7. Quoted in John Forster, *Life of Charles Dickens,* rev. J. W. T. Ley (London: 1928), 611.
8. Austin Olney, telephone interview with author, 3 December 1997.

Chapter Four

1. Scott O'Dell, *The King's Fifth* (Boston: Houghton Mifflin, 1966), 4; hereafter cited in text as *Fifth.*
2. John Rowe Townsend, *A Sense of Story: Essays on Contemporary Writers for Children* (Philadelphia: Lippincott, 1971), 156.
3. Review of *The King's Fifth,* by Scott O'Dell, *Virginia Kirkus' Service,* 1 September 1966, 913.
4. Scott O'Dell, *The Black Pearl* (Boston: Houghton Mifflin, 1967), 18; hereafter cited in text as *Pearl.*
5. Scott O'Dell, *Sing Down the Moon* (Boston: Houghton Mifflin, 1970), 30; hereafter cited in text as *Sing.*

6. Betty Baker, review of *Sing Down the Moon,* by Scott O'Dell, *New York Times Book Review,* 18 October 1970, 34.

7. Zena Sutherland, review of *Sing Down the Moon,* by Scott O'Dell, *Bulletin of the Center for Children's Books* (January 1971): 78.

8. Scott O'Dell, *Zia* (Boston: Houghton Mifflin, 1976), 85–86; hereafter cited in text as *Zia.*

9. Isabel Quigly, "Child of the Sun," review of *Zia,* by Scott O'Dell, *Times Literary Supplement,* 15 July 1977, 860.

10. Bernard DeVoto, *The Year of Decision: 1846* (Boston: Little, Brown, 1943), 357.

11. Denise M. Wilms, review of *Carlota,* by Scott O'Dell, *Booklist,* 1 October 1977, 300.

12. Ruth M. Stein, review of *Carlota,* by Scott O'Dell, *Language Arts* (April 1978): 523.

Chapter Five

1. Scott O'Dell, *The Dark Canoe* (Boston: Houghton Mifflin, 1968), 165.

2. Scott O'Dell, "Acceptance Speech: Hans Christian Andersen Award," *Horn Book Magazine* (October 1972): 443.

3. Robert Hood, review of *The Dark Canoe,* by Scott O'Dell, *New York Times Book Review,* 3 November 1968, pt. 2, 22.

4. Sarah Congdon, "Del Mar Writer O'dell [sic] Explores Metaphysical World in *Dark Canoe,*" *La Jolla Light and La Jolla Journal,* 28 November 1968.

5. Digby B. Whitman, review of *The Dark Canoe,* by Scott O'Dell, *Washington Post,* 3 November 1968, Book World section, pt. 2, 12.

6. "Brothers at Sea," review of *The Dark Canoe,* by Scott O'Dell, *Times Literary Supplement,* 4 December 1969, 1390.

7. Scott O'Dell, *The Treasure of Topo-El-Bampo* (Boston: Houghton Mifflin, 1972), 35; hereafter cited in text as *Treasure.*

8. Paul Heins, review of *The Treasure of Topo-El-Bampo,* by Scott O'Dell, *Horn Book Magazine* (June 1972): 265.

9. Zena Sutherland, review of *The Treasure of Topo-El-Bampo,* by Scott O'Dell, *Bulletin of the Center for Children's Books* (May 1972): 144.

10. Scott O'Dell, *The Cruise of the Arctic Star* (Boston: Houghton Mifflin, 1973), 69; hereafter cited in text as *Cruise.*

11. Elizabeth Hall, telephone interview with author, 17 December 1996.

Chapter Six

1. Scott O'Dell, *The Captive* (Boston: Houghton Mifflin, 1979), 43; hereafter cited in text as *Captive.*

2. Nancy Berkowitz, review of *The Captive*, by Scott O'Dell, *Children's Literature Review*, vol. 16, ed. Gerard J. Senick (Detroit: Gale, 1989), 174. First published in *School Library Journal* 26 (November 1979): 92.

3. Review of *The Captive*, by Scott O'Dell, *Children's Literature Review*, vol. 16, ed. Gerard J. Senick (Detroit: Gale, 1989), 174. First published in *Kirkus Reviews*, 15 January 1980, 71.

4. John Warren Stewig, "A Literary and Linguistic Analysis of Scott O'Dell's *The Captive*," *Children's Literature Association Quarterly* 14 (Fall 1989): 135–38.

5. Leon Garfield, "Young Man among the Mayans," review of *The Captive*, by Scott O'Dell, *Children's Literature Review*, vol. 16, ed. Gerard J. Senick (Detroit: Gale, 1989), 175. First published in *Washington Post*, 9 March 1980, Book World section, 7.

6. Scott O'Dell, *The Feathered Serpent* (Boston: Houghton Mifflin, 1981), 97.

7. Georgess McHargue, review of *The Feathered Serpent*, by Scott O'Dell, *Children's Literature Review*, vol. 16, ed. Gerard J. Senick (Detroit: Gale, 1989), 177. First published in *New York Times Book Review*, 10 January 1982, 26.

8. Scott O'Dell, "The Tribulations of a Trilogy," *Horn Book Magazine* 58 (April 1982): 143; hereafter cited in text as "Tribulations."

9. Scott O'Dell, *The Amethyst Ring* (Boston: Houghton Mifflin, 1983), 29; hereafter cited in text as *Amethyst*.

Chapter Seven

1. Richard Bradford, quoted in "Scott O'Dell," in *Contemporary Literary Criticism*, vol. 30, ed. Jean C. Stine and Daniel G. Marowski (Detroit: Gale, 1984), 271.

2. Scott O'Dell, *Child of Fire* (Boston: Houghton Mifflin, 1974), 212; hereafter cited in text as *Child*.

3. "Scott O'Dell," *Children's Literature Review*, vol. 16, ed. Gerard J. Senick (Detroit: Gale, 1989), 170–71; hereafter cited in text as Senick.

4. Paul Heins, quoted in "Scott O'Dell," in *Contemporary Literary Criticism*, vol. 30, ed. Jean C. Stine and Daniel G. Marowski (Detroit: Gale, 1984), 271.

5. Sally Rumbaugh, review of *Kathleen, Please Come Home*, by Scott O'Dell, *World of Children's Books* 3, no. 2 (1978): 75; hereafter cited in text.

6. Scott O'Dell, *Kathleen, Please Come Home* (Boston: Houghton Mifflin, 1978), 62–63.

7. Margaret Loke, "Splitting Is Hard," review of *Kathleen, Please Come Home*, by Scott O'Dell, *New York Times Book Review*, 30 April 1978, 53.

8. Scott O'Dell, *The Spanish Smile* (Boston: Houghton Mifflin, 1982), 94.

9. Craig Shaw Gardner, "Fantasy to Cut Your Teeth On," review of *The Spanish Smile,* by Scott O'Dell, *Washington Post,* 9 January 1983, Book World section, 11.

10. Patty S. Harber, review of *The Castle in the Sea,* by Scott O'Dell, *Voices of Youth Advocates* 7 (April 1984): 34.

11. Sally Estes, review of *The Castle in the Sea,* by Scott O'Dell, *Booklist,* 15 September 1983, 160.

12. Barbara Chatton, review of *Alexandra,* by Scott O'Dell, *School Library Journal* 30 (August 1984): 86.

13. Karen Stang Hanley, review of *Alexandra,* by Scott O'Dell, *Booklist,* 15 May 1984, 1345–46.

14. Scott O'Dell, *Alexandra* (Boston: Houghton Mifflin, 1984), 113.

15. Scott O'Dell, *Black Star, Bright Dawn* (Boston: Houghton Mifflin, 1988), 19; hereafter cited in text as *Black.*

Chapter Eight

1. Scott O'Dell, *Sarah Bishop* (Boston: Houghton Mifflin, 1980), 89; hereafter cited in text as *Sarah.*

2. Jean Fritz, review of *Sarah Bishop,* by Scott O'Dell, *New York Times Book Review,* 4 May 1980, 26.

3. Review of *The Road to Damietta,* by Scott O'Dell, *Publishers Weekly,* 1 November 1985, 66.

4. Scott O'Dell, *The Road to Damietta* (Boston: Houghton Mifflin, 1985), 227; hereafter cited in text as *Road.*

5. Review of *The Road to Damietta,* by Scott O'Dell, *Bulletin of the Center for Children's Books* 39 (December 1985): 74.

6. Geoff Fox, "Moments of Truth," *Times Educational Supplement,* 3 February 1978, 36.

7. Scott O'Dell, *Streams to the River, River to the Sea: A Novel of Sacagewea* (Boston: Houghton Mifflin, 1986), 72; hereafter cited in text as *Streams.*

8. Frank Bergon, ed., *The Journals of Lewis and Clark* (New York: Penguin, 1989), 88.

9. Scott O'Dell, *The Serpent Never Sleeps: A Novel of Jamestown and Pocahontas* (Boston: Houghton Mifflin, 1987), 16; hereafter cited in text as *Serpent.*

10. Scott O'Dell, *My Name Is Not Angelica* (Boston: Houghton Mifflin, 1989), 18.

11. Scott O'Dell (with Elizabeth Hall), *Thunder Rolling in the Mountains* (Boston: Houghton Mifflin, 1992), 5; hereafter cited in text as *Thunder.*

Chapter Nine

1. Scott O'Dell, *The Hawk That Dare Not Hunt by Day* (Boston: Houghton Mifflin, 1975), 183.

2. Lois R. Kuznets, "Henry James and the Storyteller: The Development of a Central Consciousness in Realistic Fiction for Children," in *The Voice of the Narrator in Children's Literature,* ed. Charlotte F. Otten and Gary D. Schmidt (New York: Greenwood Press, 1989), 189; hereafter cited in text.

3. Avrom Fleishman, *The English Historical Novel: Walter Scott to Virginia Woolf* (Baltimore: Johns Hopkins University Press, 1971), 4.

4. Scott O'Dell, "Newbery Award Acceptance," Horn Book Magazine (August 1961): 316.

5. Isabel Schon, "A Master Storyteller and His Distortion of Pre-Columbian and Hispanic Cultures," *Journal of Reading* 29 (January 1986): 323; hereafter cited in text.

6. Beverly Slapin and Doris Seale, *Through Indian Eyes: The Native American Experience in Books for Children* (Philadelphia: New Society, 1992), 197.

7. Ellen Sallé, "Ethnicity and Authenticity, or: How Black (Hispanic, Native American, Etc.) Do I Gotta Be?" *Emergency Librarian* 22 (November/December 1994): 24; hereafter cited in text.

8. Henry Louis Gates Jr., " 'Authenticity,' or, the Lesson of Little Tree," *New York Times,* 24 November 1991.

9. Quoted in James Higgins, "Scott O'Dell," in *Twentieth-Century Children's Writers,* 3d ed., ed. Tracy Chevalier (Chicago: St. James Press, 1989), 736.

Selected Bibliography

PRIMARY WORKS

Books

Alexandra. Boston: Houghton Mifflin, 1984.

The Amethyst Ring. Boston: Houghton Mifflin, 1983.

The Black Pearl. Boston: Houghton Mifflin, 1967.

Black Star, Bright Dawn. Boston: Houghton Mifflin, 1988.

The Captive. Boston: Houghton Mifflin, 1979.

Carlota. Boston: Houghton Mifflin, 1977. Published in Great Britain as *The Daughter of Don Saturnino.* Oxford: Oxford University Press, 1979.

The Castle in the Sea. Boston: Houghton Mifflin, 1983.

Child of Fire. Boston: Houghton Mifflin, 1974.

Country of the Sun: Southern California, an Informal Guide. New York: Crowell, 1957.

The Cruise of the Arctic Star. Boston: Houghton Mifflin, 1973.

The Dark Canoe. Boston: Houghton Mifflin, 1968.

The Feathered Serpent. Boston: Houghton Mifflin, 1981.

The Hawk That Dare Not Hunt by Day. Boston: Houghton Mifflin, 1975.

Hill of the Hawk. Indianapolis: Bobbs-Merrill, 1947.

Island of the Blue Dolphins. Boston: Houghton Mifflin, 1960.

Journey to Jericho. Boston: Houghton Mifflin, 1969.

Kathleen, Please Come Home. Boston: Houghton Mifflin, 1978.

The King's Fifth. Boston: Houghton Mifflin, 1966.

Man Alone, by William Doyle with Scott O'Dell. Indianapolis: Bobbs-Merrill, 1953. Published in Great Britain as *Lifer.* London: Longmans Green, 1954.

My Name Is Not Angelica. Boston: Houghton Mifflin, 1989.

The Psychology of Children's Art, by Rhoda Kellogg with Scott O'Dell. New York: CRM-Random House, 1967.

Representative Photoplays Analyzed: Modern Authorship. Hollywood, Calif.: Palmer Institute of Authorship, 1924.

The Road to Damietta. Boston: Houghton Mifflin, 1985.

Sarah Bishop. Boston: Houghton Mifflin, 1980.

The Sea Is Red: A Novel. New York: Holt, 1958.

The Serpent Never Sleeps: A Novel of Jamestown and Pocahontas. Boston: Houghton Mifflin, 1987.

Sing Down the Moon. Boston: Houghton Mifflin, 1970.

The Spanish Smile. Boston: Houghton Mifflin, 1982.

Streams to the River, River to the Sea: A Novel of Sacagawea. Boston: Houghton Mifflin, 1986.

Thunder Rolling in the Mountains (with Elizabeth Hall). Boston: Houghton Mifflin, 1992.

The Treasure of Topo-el-Bampo. Boston: Houghton Mifflin, 1972.

The 290. Boston: Houghton Mifflin, 1986.

Woman of Spain: A Story of Old California. Boston: Houghton Mifflin, 1934.

Zia. Boston: Houghton Mifflin, 1976.

Articles

"Acceptance Speech: Hans Christian Andersen Award." *Horn Book Magazine* (October 1972): 441–43.

"An Embarrassing Plenty: Writers Resolve the Problem by Evading It." *Saturday Review,* 30 October 1943, 5.

"Books Remembered." *The Calendar* 34 (Fall/Winter 1975–1976).

"Dignity of the Human Spirit." In *Children's Authors Speak,* ed. Jeanine L. Laughlin and Sherry Laughlin. Englewood, Colo.: Libraries Unlimited, 1993.

"History and Fiction." *Five Owls* 3 (January/February 1990): 33–35.

"Responses Came by the Thousands." *San Francisco Sunday Examiner,* 5 November 1967, 40, 42.

"Scott O'Dell." In *Speaking for Ourselves: Autobiographical Sketches by Notable Authors of Books for Young Adults,* comp. and ed. Donald R. Gallo. Urbana, Ill.: National Council of Teachers of English, 1990.

"So Now They Say: 'He Wrote a Book.' " *Los Angeles Times Sunday Magazine,* 13 May 1934, 94.

"The Tribulations of a Trilogy." *Horn Book Magazine* (April 1982): 137–44.

SECONDARY SOURCES

Reviews and Criticism

"Authors and Editors." *Publishers' Weekly,* 15 November 1971, 21–23.

Cain, Bill. "Children's Authors Honored." *Times-Advocate,* 30 March 1972.

Congdon, Sarah. "Del Mar Writer O'dell {sic} Explores Metaphysical World in *Dark Canoe.*" *La Jolla Light and La Jolla Journal,* 28 November 1968.

DeLuca, Geraldine. "Unself-Conscious Voices: Larger Contexts for Adolescents." *The Lion and the Unicorn* 2 (Fall 1978): 89–108.

Fleishman, Avrom. *The English Historical Novel: Walter Scott to Virginia Woolf.* Baltimore: Johns Hopkins University Press, 1971.

Fox, Geoff. "Moments of Truth." *Times Educational Supplement,* 3 February 1978, 36.

Gates, Henry Louis Jr. " 'Authenticity,' or, the Lesson of Little Tree." *New York Times* 24 November 1991.

Hannabuss, Stuart. "Islands as Metaphors." *Universities Quarterly* 38 (Winter 1983–1984): 70–82.

"He Writes Up to Children." *Kona Kai Club Islander* 1 (April 1970): 23.

Higgins, James E. "Scott O'Dell." In *Twentieth-Century Children's Writers,* 3d ed, ed. Tracy Chevalier. Chicago: St. James Press, 1989.

Hopkins, Lee Bennett. "Lee Bennett Hopkins Interviews Scott O'Dell." In *Star Walk,* ed. P. David Pearson et al. Needham, Mass: Silver Burdett & Ginn, 1989.

Kuznets, Lois. "Henry James and the Storyteller: The Development of a Central Consciousness in Realistic Fiction for Children." In *The Voice of the Narrator in Children's Literature,* ed. Charlotte F. Otten and Gary D. Schmidt. New York: Greenwood Press, 1989.

Lovelace, Maud Hart. "Scott O'Dell." *Horn Book Magazine* (August 1961): 316–19.

Lukacs, Georg. *The Historical Novel,* trans. Hannah Mitchell and Stanley Mitchell. Boston: Beacon, 1963.

Lundin, Anne H. "The Legacy of Robinson Crusoe." *Five Owls* 2 (January/February 1988): 33–36.

Maher, Susan Naramore. "Encountering Others: The Meeting of Cultures in Scott O'Dell's *Island of the Blue Dolphins* and *Sing Down the Moon.*" *Children's Literature in Education* 23, no. 4 (1992): 215–27.

McCormick, Edith. "Scott O'Dell: Immortal Writer." *American Libraries* 4 (June 1973): 356–57.

Mingshui, Cai. "Variables and Values in Historical Fiction for Children." *The New Advocate* 5 (Fall 1992): 279–91.

Roop, Peter. "Profile: Scott O'Dell." *Language Arts* 61 (November 1984): 750–52.

Sallé, Ellen. "Ethnicity and Authenticity, or: How Black (Hispanic, Native American, Etc.) Do I Gotta Be?" *Emergency Librarian* 22, no. 2 (1994): 22–27.

Schon, Isabel. "A Master Storyteller and His Distortions of Pre-Columbian and Hispanic Cultures." *Journal of Reading* 29 (January 1986): 322–25.

"Scott O'Dell." In *Children's Literature Review,* vol. 1, ed. Ann Block and Carolyn Riley. Detroit: Gale, 1976.

"Scott O'Dell." In *Children's Literature Review,* vol. 16, ed. Gerard J. Senick. Detroit: Gale, 1989.

"Scott O'Dell" In *Contemporary Literary Criticism,* vol. 30, ed. Jean C. Stine and Daniel G. Marowski. Detroit: Gale, 1984.

"Scott O'Dell" In *Something about the Author,* vol. 12, ed. Anne Commire. Detroit: Gale, 1977.

"Scott O'Dell." In *Something about the Author,* vol. 60, ed. Anne Commire. Detroit: Gale, 1990.

Slapin, Beverly, and Doris Seale. *Through Indian Eyes: The Native American Experience in Books for Children.* Philadelphia: New Society, 1992.

Stewig, John Warren. "A Literary and Linguistic Analysis of Scott O'Dell's *The Captive.*" *Children's Literature Association Quarterly* 14 (Fall 1989): 135–38.

Stott, Jon C. "Narrative Technique and Meaning in *Island of the Blue Dolphins.*" *Elementary English* 52 (April 1975): 442–46.

Thompson, Sally Anne M. "Scott O'Dell: Weaver of Stories." *Catholic Library World* (March 1978): 340–42.

Townsend, John Rowe. *A Sense of Story: Essays on Contemporary Writers for Children.* Philadelphia: Lippincott, 1971.

Trzebinski, Errol. *The Lives of Beryl Markham.* New York: Norton, 1993.

Usrey, Malcolm. "Scott O'Dell." *Dictionary of Literary Biography,* vol. 52, *American Writers for Children Since 1960: Fiction,* ed. Glenn E. Estes. Detroit: Gale, 1986.

Wesselhoeft, Conrad. "*Blue Dolphins'* Author Tells Why He Writes for Children." *New York Times,* 15 April 1984.

Wintle, Justin. "Scott O'Dell Interviewed by Justin Wintle." In *The Pied Pipers: Interviews with the Influential Creators of Children's Literature,* by Justin Wintle and Emma Fisher. New York: Paddington Press, 1974.

Index

The Author

David L. Russell holds a Ph.D. in Renaissance literature and is a professor at Ferris State University where he teaches children's and adolescent literature. In addition to numerous published articles on the subject of children's literature, he has written a textbook, *Literature for Children* (Longman), now going into its fourth edition, and has contributed to the *Dictionary of Literary Biography* and the forthcoming *Cambridge Guide to Children's Literature*. He is the author of *Patricia MacLachlan*, a publication of the Twayne United States Author series. A past member of the Board of Directors of the Children's Literature Association, he currently serves as the Association's Publications Chair.

The Editor

Ruth K. MacDonald is college dean for the I Have a Dream Foundation in Hartford, Connecticut. She received her B.A. and M.A. in English from the University of Connecticut, her Ph.D. in English from Rutgers University, and her M.B.A. from the University of Texas at El Paso. She is the author of the volumes on Louisa May Alcott, Beatrix Potter, and Dr. Seuss in Twayne's United States Authors and English Authors series and of the books *Literature for Children in England and America, 1646–1774* (1982) and *Christian's Children: The Influence of John Bunyan's "Pilgrim's Progress" on American Children's Literature* (1989).